The Top 5 Most Famous Queens: Nefertiti, Cleopatra, Elizabeth I, Catherine the Great, and Queen Victoria

By Charles River Editors

About Charles River Editors

Charles River Editors was founded by Harvard and MIT alumni to provide superior editing and original writing services, with the expertise to create digital content for publishers across a vast range of subject matter. In addition to providing original digital content for third party publishers, Charles River Editors republishes civilization's greatest literary works, bringing them to a new generation via ebooks.

Visit charlesrivereditors.com for more information.

The famous bust of Nefertiti

Nefertiti (circa 1370-1330 B.C.)

In the early 20th century, over 3,000 years after her death, Nefertiti became a household name across the world and one of the most famous women of the ancient world. Egyptologists were aware that she was a queen of the New Kingdom Egypt during the later portion of the 18th dynasty, but she was little known until the presentation of a reconstructed bust depicting her at the Berlin Museum in 1924. Nefertiti means "the beautiful one has come", and if the presented bust is anything to judge by she, was indeed a beautiful woman.

The bust of Nefertiti caused an enormous sensation following the glamorous discovery of the tomb of Tutankhamen in 1922 by Howard Carter. The bust was the work of the ancient royal sculptor Thutmose and was first discovered by German archaeologists in a fragmented state in the remains of Thutmose's workshop at the ancient city of Akhetaten, known today as Tell el-Amarna. With the discovery and display of the bust, the once little known queen Nefertiti became eponymous with Ancient Egypt, alongside that of the Great Pyramids at Giza and the Golden Funerary Mask of the young Tutankhamen. And thanks to that bust, Nefertiti's image has become immortalized and may be found in replica busts, earrings, necklaces, paintings and seemingly every other artificat that can be found at an Egyptian vendors shop.

But what about the actual woman represented by that bust? As it turned out, far from being an inconsequential queen, Nefertiti may have been an important wife of Akhenaten, whose reign marked the first time Egyptians practiced monotheistic beliefs by worshipping one god, the sun-disc Aten. Ironically, Akhenaten's revolutionary and influential reign has long been obscured by one of his wives and one of his sons, Tutankhamen.

Despite the artifacts found and the fascination with Nefertiti and Tutankhamen, there is still plenty of uncertainty and mystery surrounding the Egyptian queen. What life did such a hauntingly beautiful woman live? Where was she from? Did a queen sometimes labeled "Lordess of the Two Lands" in ancient artifacts rule Egypt, and if so, when and why? How did she die? Despite her recent fame she is still a relatively enigmatic historical figure, with fragments of her life still being pieced together by historians over the last century.

The Top 5 Most Famous Queens looks at the known and unknown about the Ancient Egyptian queen and attempts to separate fact from fiction to analyze her life and reign. Along with pictures and a bibliography, you will learn about Nefertiti like you never have before.

Depiction of Cleopatra and Caesarion

Cleopatra (69-30 B.C.)

"Her beauty, as we are told, was in itself not altogether incomparable, nor such as to strike those who saw her; but converse with her had an irresistible charm, and her presence, combined with the persuasiveness of her discourse and the character which was somehow diffused about her behaviour towards others, had something stimulating about it. There was sweetness also in

the tones of her voice; and her tongue, like an instrument of many strings, she could readily turn to whatever language she pleased..." – Plutarch

During one of the most turbulent periods in the history of Rome, men like Julius Caesar, Mark Antony, and Octavian participated in two civil wars that would spell the end of the Roman Republic and determine who would become the Roman emperor. In the middle of it all was history's most famous woman, the Egyptian pharaoh Cleopatra (69-30 B.C.), who famously seduced both Caesar and Antony and thereby positioned herself as one of the most influential people in a world of powerful men.

Cleopatra was a legendary figure even to contemporary Romans and the ancient world, as Plutarch's quote suggests, and she was a controversial figure who was equally reviled and praised through the years, depicted as a benevolent ruler and an evil seductress, sometimes at the same time. Over 2,000 years after her death, everything about Cleopatra continues to fascinate people around the world, from her lineage as a Ptolemaic pharaoh, her physical features, the manner in which she seduced Caesar, her departure during the Battle of Actium, and her famous suicide. And despite being one of the most famous figures in history, there is still much mystery surrounding her, leading historians and archaeologists scouring Alexandria, Egypt for clues about her life and the whereabouts of her royal palace and tomb.

The Top 5 Most Famous Queens chronicles the amazing life of Egypt's most famous pharaoh, explores some of the mysteries and myths surrounding her, and analyzes her legacy, which has only grown larger over 2,000 years and promises to last many more. Along with pictures of important people, places, and events, you will learn about Cleopatra like you never have before.

Queen Elizabeth I (1533-1603)

"Video et taceo." ("I see, and say nothing") – Queen Elizabeth I

When Queen Elizabeth II came to the throne in 1952, many commentators heralded the beginning of her reign as the second Elizabethan age. The first one, of course, concerned the reign of Henry VIII's second surviving daughter and middle surviving child, Queen Elizabeth I, one of England's most famous and influential rulers. It was an age when the arts, commerce and trade flourished. It was the epoch of gallantry and great, enduring literature. It was also an age of wars and military conflicts in which men were the primary drivers and women often were pawns.

Elizabeth I changed the rules of the game and indeed she herself was changed by the game. She was a female monarch of England, a kingdom that had unceremoniously broken with the Catholic Church, and the Vatican and the rest of Christendom was baying for her blood. She had had commercial and militaristic enemies galore. In the end, she helped change the entire structure of female leadership.

Elizabeth was the last Tudor sovereign, the daughter of the cruel and magnificent King Henry VIII and a granddaughter of the Tudor House's founder, the shrewd Henry VII. Elizabeth, hailed as "Good Queen Bess," "Gloriana" and "The Virgin Queen" to this day in the public firmament, would improve upon Henry VIII's successes and mitigate his failures, and despite her own failings would turn out to "have the heart and stomach of a king, and a king of England too". Indeed, that was the phrase she would utter in describing herself while exhorting her troops to fight for England against the Spanish Armada).

Elizabeth often has been featured in biographies that were more like hagiographies, glossing over her fits of temper, impatience and other frailties. It is fair to say, however, that she had also inherited her grandfather's political acumen and her father's magnificence, thus creating not just one of the most colourful courts in Europe but also one of the most effective governments in English history. It was an age of Christopher Marlowe's and William Shakespeare's flourishing creativity that still enhances English as well as comparative literature. Elizabeth was also patroness of Sir Francis Drake, the pirate, thereby promoting English settlement of foreign colonies. The Jamestown Settlement in Virginia would come in 1607, four years after Elizabeth's passing, and the Plymouth colony in Massachusetts would come in 1620.

Elizabeth had also fought for her life time and time again in an era that was already unsafe for female leaders and she probably had remembered the searing feeling of realizing that her mother Queen Anne (Anne Boleyn) had been executed by her father arguably on a trumped-up charge. Danger was pervasive; strategy was needed not just to thrive but just to survive.

The Top 5 Most Famous Queens chronicles the life and reign of England's most famous queen, but it also humanizes the woman who ruled one of the world's most powerful kingdoms in an age dominated by men. Along with pictures of important people, places, and events in her life, you will learn about Elizabeth I like you never have before.

Catherine the Great (1729-1796)

"This princess seems to combine every kind of ambition in her person. Everything that may add luster to her reign will have some attraction for her. Science and the arts will be encouraged to flourish in the empire, projects useful for the domestic economy will be undertaken. She will endeavor to reform the administration of justice and to invigorate the laws; but her policies will be based on Machiavellianism; and I should not be surprised if in this field she rivals the king of Prussia. She will adopt the prejudices of her entourage regarding the superiority of her power and will endeavor to win respect not by the sincerity and probity of her actions but also by an ostentatious display of her strength. Haughty as she is, she will stubbornly pursue her undertakings and will rarely retrace a false step. Cunning and falsity appear to be vices in her character; woe to him who puts too much trust in her. Love affairs may become a stumbling block to her ambition and prove fatal for her peace of mind. This passionate princess, still held in check by the fear and consciousness of internal troubles, will know no restraint once she believes herself firmly established." - Baron de Breteuil

As one of the most famous women rulers in history, Russian Empress Catherine the Great has long been remembered not only as one of the most powerful women of her time, but she was also one of the most powerful and capable rulers in all of Europe. And her path to the throne was just as remarkable as her reign.

In a story that sounds like it could have been a precursor to Cinderella, Catherine the Great was born into a family of minor nobility, but she managed to forge her own destiny through her own cunning use of diplomacy and intrigue, gradually gaining allies and power. By 1762, she confident enough to conspire against her own husband, Peter III, whose reign as Tsar lasted just six months before his arrest at the hands of his wife. Upon his arrest and death, Catherine took power as the regent for their son, Grand Duke Paul.

Despite the strong-arm tactics, Catherine came to power in the midst of the Enlightenment, which was flourishing in France and Britain, and she would rule as an Enlightened ruler. A known correspondent of Voltaire's, Catherine sought to modernize Russia and turn it into a force in its own right, creating a rich and cultured court at the same time. Over the course of nearly 35 years in power, Catherine ushered in the Russian Enlightenment and presided over a period of time known as the Golden Age of the Russian Empire.

Given her length of reign, forceful character, and lasting legacy, it was inevitable that legends about Catherine the Great would also pop up in the wake of her death. To an extent, certain legends have overshadowed her actual accomplishments, even as they continue to be circulated. *The Top 5 Most Famous Queens* addresses the controversial legends about Catherine and her reign, but it also explores how a woman became one of the most powerful rulers in a country and continent dominated by men. Along with pictures of important people, places, and events, you will learn about Catherine the Great like you never have before.

Queen Victoria (1819-1901)

"Since it has pleased Providence to place me in this station, I shall do my utmost to fulfil my duty towards my country; I am very young and perhaps in many, though not in all things, inexperienced, but I am sure that very few have more real good will and more real desire to do what is fit and right than I have." – Queen Victoria, 1837

England has had no shortage of influential monarchs, but only Queen Elizabeth I and Queen Victoria had their nation's age literally named after them. Both the Elizabethan era and Victorian era have come to symbolize a golden age of peace and progress in every aspect of British life, with the long reigns of both queens also providing stability.

Of course, there was a critical difference between those two queens: Elizabeth I still wielded great power in the 16th century, whereas Victoria was a constitutional monarch with limited power over the workings of the British government. But in a way, that made Victoria even more unique, as she still proved able to mold the cultural identity of a nearly 65 year long epoch. Furthermore, Victoria established some of the ceremonial customs of the British monarch and became both the forerunner and role model of subsequent queens, a legacy that continues to endure with her great-great granddaughter, Queen Elizabeth II.

Though Britain's longest reigning monarch is now mostly associated with conservative values (particularly strict morality and traditional social and gender roles), Victoria and her era oversaw the cultural and technological progress of Britain and the West in general, architectural revivals, and the expansion of imperialism. While some of these developments have been perceived negatively over a century later, Britons of the 19th century and early 20th century often viewed the Victorian Era as the height of their nation's power and influence.

The Top 5 Most Famous Queens chronicles the life and reign of Queen Victoria, while examining the enduring legacy of the era in British history named after her. Along with pictures of important people, places, and events in her life, you will learn about Queen Victoria like you never have before.

Nefertiti
Chapter 1: The 18th Dynasty

The 18th Dynasty of the New Kingdom of Ancient Egypt was a time of prosperity, growth, and military dominance, and Egyptologists have settled on the dates 1550-1292 B.C. as being the era of that dynasty. Thanks in no small part to Nefertiti herself, she lived during the 18th dynasty's most famous epoch as queen alongside Amenhotep IV/Akhenaten from circa 1352-1336 B.C. Akhenaten's reign ended only 41 years before the end of the nearly 260 year long dynasty, and Nefertiti herself may have numbered among the 13-15 rulers of the 18th Dynasty after Akhenaten's reign. The 18th Dynasty heralded the New Kingdom period of Ancient Egypt's history.

Egyptologists refer to this period as the New Kingdom because the reigns of these rulers completely transformed the kingdom's borders and culture. The Egyptian kingdom's boundaries were stretched further than they had ever been before, and at the time same time Egyptian society flourished, with literature, architecture, art and wealth all reaching new heights. Amenhotep I, Thutmose III, Hatshepsut, Akhenaten, Tutankhamen, Ramses the Great and Sety I were some of the most powerful, influential, and controversial rulers Egypt ever had, and all of them reigned during the New Kingdom, most from the 18th dynasty. The list of 18th dynasty rulers was as follows:

Ahmose (1550-1525)
Amenhotep I (1525-1504)
Thutmose I (1504-1492)
Thutmose II (1492-1479)
Thutmose III (1479-1425)
Hatshepsut (1473-1458)
Amenhotep II (1427-1400)
Thutmose IV (1400-1390)
Amenhotep III (1390-1352)
Amenhotep IV/Akhenaten (1352-1336)
Smenkhare (?)
Nefemeferuaten (who some scholars believe was Nefertiti) (?)
Tutankhamen (1336-1327)
Ay (1327-1323)
Horemheb (1323-1295)

The 18th dynasty began with a man named Ahomse. Previous to the New Kingdom, Egypt was in an intermediate period, during which the country was not unified by a single ruler. It began with internal strife and decline, but it coalesced into a single entity following the invasion of the Hyksos, who ruled Egypt during the 15th, 16th, and 17th dynasties. The following is an excerpt from Manetho's Aegyptiaca describing the invasion and rule of the Hyksos.

"...for what cause I know not, a blast of God smote us; and unexpectedly, from the regions of the East, invaders of obscure race marched in confidence of victory against our land. By main force they easily overpowered the rulers of the land, they then burned our cities ruthlessly, razed to the ground the temples of the gods, and treated all the natives with a cruel hostility, massacring some and leading into slavery the wives and children of others. Finally, they appointed as king one of their number whose name was Salitis. He had his seat at Memphis, levying tribute from Upper and Lower Egypt, and leaving garrisons behind in the most advantageous positions. Above all, he fortified the district to the east, foreseeing that the Assyrians, as they grew stronger, would one day covet and attack his kingdom."

The Hyksos mostly controlled the northern regions of the country, using the city of Avaris as their political center, but they also retained a strong influence over the southern regions of Egypt through taxation of the ruling Theban princes. Despite what the ancient historian Manetho would have us believe, the Hyksos were not tyrannical rulers. However, during the 17th dynasty they began to appoint more and more foreign administrators, which caused unrest amongst the people.

Additionally, they may have begun to impose higher taxes. Whatever the ultimate causes, there was conflict between the Theban princes and the Hyksos. Ahmose was the last of three 17th dynasty rulers, Tao and Kamose being his predecessors, and he was responsible for freeing the Egyptian peoples form the yoke of the Hyksos. He spent his life fighting them, and it was not until the end of his reign that he succeeded in re-unifying Egypt. With the reunification, Egypt heralded in a new dynasty, and a New Kingdom. Egypt had changed from being a brilliant but insular nation, to one with a strong standing army that was ready to expand and defend Egypt's borders. Egypt found itself interacting on a much larger diplomatic and foreign scale than it ever had before.

Statue of Ahmose I

Egypt during the 18th Dynasty saw its capital being centralized in Thebes (modern day Luxor), with major cities and military bases spread throughout the North in the Delta region. The god Amen gained great prominence and acquired new roles as a god of fertility and warfare, and he was soon tied in with the sun god Ra, forming the god Amen-Ra. The early rulers of the dynasty were focused strongly upon their military prowess, and they succeeded in expanding Egypt's borders in the north into the Levant, including parts of modern Syria and Israel. In the south, they pressed their interests and control over the Nubians, located in southern Egypt and northern Sudan. They were the makers of Egypt's first empire. The legendary military prowess of Thutmose I was only surpassed by that of his grandson Thutmose III, who undertook 14 campaigns in the Levant in order to subdue it. Egypt would not see its expansion surpassed until the Rameside period.

Social and cultural changes were also brought about during the New Kingdom. A new burial site was chosen for its rulers, across the banks from Thebes; first in the area around Dra Abu el-Naga, which was used by 17th dynasty princes, and then later in the Valley of the Kings. The tomb-workers' village of Deir el-Bahri is thought to have been founded by Amenhotep I, the second ruler of the 18th dynasty, and his mother Ahmose-Nefertari. Art and literature flourished under the reign of Queen Hatshepsut, who was arguably Egypt's most powerful and influential female ruler. She began her reign ostensibly as the regent of Thutmoses III, but she quickly took on kingly titles and ruled in her own right for many years until Thutmoses III decided to take control.

Not long after the reign of Thutmose III, Egypt's borders ceased expansion and focused on consolidation during the reign of Amenhotep III. Amenhotep III brought control to the region through diplomacy rather than through arms, and it is believed that Nefertiti was born during his rule. If so, it means Nefertiti lived her early life during his reign, and it was upon his death that she became Egypt's queen as the Great Wife of one of Ancient Egypt's most famous rulers, Amenhotep IV/Akhenaten, Egypt's so called 'heretic' king.

Chapter 2: Akhenaten

Statue of Akhenaten

Akhenaten was born Amenhotep, the younger son of king Amenhotep III and of queen Tiy. He was one of six or seven known children by Amenhotep III and Tiy, and his birth relegated him to a secondary position in the royal family during his early childhood. The crown prince Thutmose and the princesses Sitamen, Henut-Taneb, Isis, and Nebetah preceded his own birth. While many of the dates of birth of Akhenaten and his siblings are not known for sure, it is clear that he was one of the youngest amongst them. A hereditary king's early life could often be easily traced in Ancient Egypt, but this was not so in the case of Akhenaten. Being born a younger son, he would have never held a position of prominence within the immediate royal family and therefore his name could not be expected to be found in inscriptions.

Conversely, his elder brother Thutmose's earlier years are documented to some degree. It is known that after Thutmose's early education, he was inured at Memphis, where he would have been expected to gain further training in the running of the Egyptian state. Memphis was the administrative capital of Ancient Egypt and the center of the cult for the god Ptah. While Thutmose was there, he was at some point granted the position of *sem*-priest of the god Ptah, a common practice among the kings of the 18th Dynasty and among the Rameside kings. There are a handful of inscriptions pertaining to Thutmose, some of which indicate that he was given rights over the burial of the Apis bulls in Memphis, but little else is known about Thutmose's life. This has led to speculation that he may have died young, possibly in year 30 of the reign of Amenhotep III, and he possibly may have been buried in Saqqara outside of Memphis. No tomb for him has ever been discovered.

It was Thutmose's early demise that lead to Akhenaten's rise in fortunes. The only record of the transition is a small disputed graffito found in the mortuary temple of the pyramid at Meidum, which some believe recorded the crowning of Amenhotep IV in year 30 of the reign of Amenhotep III. Of all the children of Amenhotep III and Tiy, the one whose name occurs the most during the reign of Amenhotep III is Sitamen. It seems to have been more common for the 18th Dynasty rulers to depict their daughters rather than their sons on artifacts, but either way it's apparent that Sitamen held a position of preference. She was referred to as "the eldest daughter of the king, whom he loves", and given lands, privileges, and titles that clearly indicated she was a favored child of Amenhotep III. She even reached the rank of "Great King's Wife", though it is very doubtful that she ever outshone her mother in both power, and influence within the court and with Amenhotep III.

Their mother, queen Tiy, is one of Egypt's more famous queens, and she had a remarkable amount of power granted upon her. The 18th dynasty was not short on powerful, influential woman, especially with Queen Hatshepsut ranked among their numbers. Hatshepsut, who reigned as regent on behalf of her step-son Thutmose III, went so far as to give herself kingly titles and to have herself depicted in the time honored visage of a king, being adorned with symbols of kingship. It seems she ruled Egypt from about 1473-1458 B.C. on her step-son's behalf, and she did so with seemingly no strain between herself and Thutmose III.

Tiy was the proudly proclaimed daughter of Thuya and Yuya, and her mother Thuya had few qualms about declaring their relationship in her tomb. Tiy would have been very young when she married Amenhotep III, around 12-13 years old, and Amenhotep III had come to Egypt's throne at a very young age. While he was still in his teens, his mother Mutemwia reigned in his stead as regent, but Mutemwia's position of dominance quickly faded when Tiy became queen. Early historians often described Tiy as being "common" or of low birth because she was not a member of the royal family, but she proved to be anything but common. Tiy's parents were clearly of the Egyptians elite class; Tiy's father held the tittles "One trusted by the Gods", "Foremost of the companions of the Kings", "Overseer of the King's horses" and "God's Father'. Amenhotep was not in the least ashamed of Tiy's parentage; in fact, he proudly proclaimed it upon their union. The following is from an inscription found on one of the commemorative scarabs that were commissioned by Amenhotep III: "King of Upper and Lower Egypt, Nebmaatre, son of Re, Amenhotep ruler of Thebes, given life, and the king's principal wife Tiy, may she live. The name of her father is Yuya and the name of her mother is Thuya; she is the wife of a mighty king…"

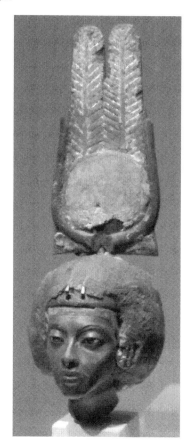

Statue of Tiy

Tiy has never been historically considered a great beauty, especially in comparison with her successor Nefertiti. The images that exist of Tiy depict a woman with almost severe features, noted by her pinched lips, and Tiy's race has often been questioned by scholars due to the inconsistent coloring found in some of the sculptures and relief images of her. In some she is depicted as a light skinned woman, but in others she is depicted with very dark skin. But this in itself might not be remarkable and could simply be a reflection of the pieces either being commissioned before or after her death, with the dark skin being representative of the green or black skin of the god Osiris. There is a bust of Tiy in the Berlin Museum that is carved from a dark wood, which has given rise to the theory that she may have been a Nubian woman, but there are no Nubian features to be found in the mummies of her parents Yuya and Thuya. Additionally, recent DNA studies have confirmed that the mummy previously identified as the "Elder Lady", which was discovered in the side chamber of KV 35 (Amenhotep II tombs), is that of queen Tiy. The DNA analysis made between the mummy, a lock of hair found in a miniature sarcophagus in the tomb of Tutankhamen bearing Tiy's name, and other previously identified mummies of the period has clearly identified the mummy as being Tiy, and of her being the daughter of Yuya and Thuya.

Tiy's power and influence rose quickly, and she was soon allocated with many prominent titles, including that of "Great King's Wife". Her name could often be found alongside that of Amenhotep III's in inscriptions, much more so than was common for a queen. She was even depicted on the same level with Amenhotep III on a colossal statue from his mortuary temple, a remarkable occurrence of great significance, because in Egyptian art the size of the figure was directly correlated with the status of the individual. By being depicted the same as the king, Tiy was depicted as his equal, something that would be seen again and further enhanced by Akhenaten and Nefertiti.

Akhenaten and Nefertiti both grew up during one of the greatest heights of Ancient Egypt's culture. Egypt was at one of its most powerful stages during the latter stages of the 18th Dynasty. Egypt was the unparalleled power of its time, and the rulers of the Middle East deferred to Egypt by sending large tribute and gifts, some of which included the sisters and daughters of the foreign monarchs, who were offered in marriage to the Egyptian king. Sons could also be sent, either out of desire to have them trained in the cultural center of the region or possibly as a form of tribute to assure the good behavior of the foreign ruler. Amenhotep III married many of the women that were offered to him in order to tighten diplomatic ties, yet he refused to allow Egyptian princesses to marry other rulers in return, which was a blatant display of Egypt's power. This is hinted at in correspondence between Amenhotep III and Kadashman-Enlil of Babylonia when he dared request the hand of an Egyptian princess: "When I wrote to you about marrying your daughter you wrote to me saying 'From time immemorial no daughter of the king of Egypt has been given into marriage to anyone.' Why did you say this? You are the king and you may do as you please. If you were to give a daughter, who would say anything about it."

The Egyptians clearly saw themselves as superior to their contemporaries, and they had no need to pander to other rulers, since their army and wealth far surpassed any of their possible rivals. Amenhotep III's ancestors had fought hard at the beginning of the 18th Dynasty to give Egypt independence and to make the country a great power, so by the time Amenhotep III reached the throne Egypt's power was consolidated and its great wealth could be turned to internal projects. Amenhotep III built vast monuments, like Amenhotep III's mortuary temple, from which only two great colossi statues remain. The Egyptian court at the time was very wealthy, and that wealth was reflected in the opulence of their lifestyle. Wealth, power, and many decades of good floods and strong crops created a world of security and decadence, and it was this time period during which Akhenaten and Nefertiti grew up,

Chapter 3: Nefertiti's Early Life

Painted limestone depicting Nefertiti and Akhenaten

Very little is known about Nefertiti's early years, or even her origins. It is not clear who her family was or even where she came from, and there are no inscriptions or letters that detail her heritage or her early life, so the details of her early life are comprised mostly of conjecture pieced together from various fragments of archaeological evidence and the historical record. Over the years historians have greatly disputed where Nefertiti came from, with two main schools of thought dividing them. The first theory holds that Nefertiti was a foreign princess, and Egyptologist Sir Flinders Petrie, one of the most eminent archaeologists of the last century, speculated that Nefertiti was the Mitannit princess Thadukhepa, sent by her father Tushratta to marry Amenhotep III. However, Amenhotep III died not long after the Mitanni princess arrived in Egypt, so she instead married Amenhotep IV/Akhenaten. The presumption is that she later changed her name to a more Egyptian one, Nefertiti. The Mitanni princess would have been of an appropriate age to be Nefertiti, and it was not unheard of for foreigners to change their names and adopt an Egyptian name. This theory is seemingly bolstered by the name Nefertiti itself, which means "the beautiful one has come", leading some historians to take the name at face value. On the other hand, other historians and scholars note that the name Nefertiti is not as unusual as first thought, and that Egyptian parents often gave their children such names with the intent of embellishing a certain trait. Thus, it is not difficult to imagine a mother wishing beauty upon her infant daughter.

The second prominent theory regarding Nefertiti's parentage and heritage posits that she may have been the daughter of Ay, who was the brother of Queen Tiy and held a number of prominent positions under the reigns of multiple kings during his life. It likely that Ay followed in the steps of his presumed father Yuya to a military career, first as a Troop Commander and later as the "Overseer of the Kings Horses". Over the years Ay rose in power, becoming a trusted advisor to Tutankhamen, and eventually taking the throne himself for four years after the death of Tutankhamen. The titles that Ay held, like "Overseer of the King's Horses" and "God's Father", were many of the same titles that Yuya had held, and there are similarities in their names. Since Ay is a derivation of the name Yuya, it is easy to assume the names are linked, connecting them as father and son. It was very common in Ancient Egypt for a son to follow in his father's path and to take on many of the same duties and titles as his father had before him. In addition to the connection found in their names and titles, Cyril Aldred has also suggested that the two men bear a resemblance to one another, noting, "There is, moreover, a close physical resemblance between these two men: It is true that we lack the body of Ay from which to draw comparisons, but the distinctive profile of Ay has been represented in various reliefs from Amarna and shows that he had the same beaky nose, thick lips, and jaw-line as Yuya's, as revealed by the latter's mummy."

Ay performing the opening of the mouth ceremony for Tutankhamen, from Tutankhamen's tomb.

In addition to these claims, there is also the connection that Ay had to Akhmim, the Ancient Egyptian town from which Yuya and Thuya hailed, and where their children would have been raised. It is in Akhmim that a temple chapel dedicated to the god Min by Ay can be found, thus providing a further connection between Ay, Yuya and Thuya. If Ay's parentage is accepted, and if he was the father of Nefertiti, that would have made Nefertiti a cousin of Akhenaten and a very respectable choice as wife and queen, perhaps even one that may have been put forth by Queen Tiy herself.

However, there is still the problem of connecting Nefertiti to Ay. The connection of the two comes through Ay's chief wife, Tey, rather than through Ay himself. Tey is believed to have been the wet-nurse of Nefertiti, and in the unfinished tomb of Tey and Ay at Akhetaten they are both shown receiving rewards of golden necklaces from King Akhenaten and Queen Nefertiti. For Tey to receive such a royal honor alongside her esteemed husband places her in a position of importance, a position further confirmed by her titles of "Favorite of the Good God", "Nurse of the King's Great Wife Nefertiti", "Nurse of the Goddess", and "Ornament of the King". These titles clearly mark lady Tey as being the wet-nurse of Nefertiti, but it remains logical conjecture that Ay was Nefertit's father.

What is clear is that Tey was not the mother of Nefertiti, given her claims to being the queen's wet-nurse; after all, why would have Tey claimed to be the wet-nurse if she had the higher claim of parentage? Nonetheless, there is substantial evidence that seems to confirm Nefertiti was an Egyptian, and that she was closely connected to the royal family and Egypt's elite class. It is very simple to take the evidence one step further and to presume that the reason Tey was Nefertiti's wet-nurse was because Nefertiti was her step-daughter, possibly the product of a previous union that had ended in the birthing of Nefertiti. It was not unusual for men to marry again, since mother and infant morality was high in Ancient Egypt even amongst the upper classes. It was also very common for women of the court to act as wet-nurses to royal children. Either way, Nefertiti would have grown up in and around the royal court of Egypt, and her position as chosen wife and Queen of Akhenaten was in no way odd or unusual.

It is believed that Nefertiti may have also had a sister who was called Mutbenret or Mutnodjmet. It is not clear whether Mutbenret was a full sister or half-sister, but she is one documented family member that appears along side Nefertiti, and she's depicted in numerous scenes of the royal family in the tombs of the elite at Akhetaten, the capital city of the Amarna Period where Nefertiti and Akhenaten resided. She is often depicted standing prominent amongst the family rather than in the background with the other ladies, and she is also labeled as "Queen's Sister". Mutbenret, like Nefertiti, never makes the claim of being a king's daughter, and like her sister, her parentage is not confirmed. Her name appears in Amarna up to the birth of Nefertiti's fourth daughter but disappears after that. The name appears again in connection with Horemheb, the successor of Ay, as his wife. She is the only known sibling, and the only known confirmed member of Nefertiti's family.

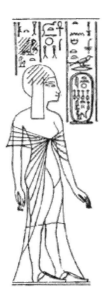

Art from a tomb depicting Mutbenret

Chapter 4: Queen of Egypt

Limestone relief of Nefertiti kissing one of her daughters,

There is no indication of what year Nefertiti was born or which year she married Amenhotep IV/Akhenaten, and therefore it is not known how old she was when they were married. However, it is relatively safe to assume that she would have been fairly young when they married, likely in her early to late teens. Confirming the date of the marriage between Nefertiti and Amenhotep IV/Akhenaten is made even more difficult by the confusion over dating the years of Amenhotep IV's reign, because there is conflicting evidence suggesting that some of his reign was spent as co-regent with his father Amenhotep III. Some speculate that they were co-regents for nearly a decade, while others believe there was no co-regency at all, but most historians today believe the co-regency was for no more than a year if at all. It is also believed that Amenhotep IV and Nefertiti were married early on during Amenhotep IV's reign, if not before. This would coincide with the birth of their first daughter Meritaten, who was believed to have been born around year 1 of Akhenaten's reign (circa 1356 B.C.).

Over the years Nefertiti bore Akhenaten 6 daughters, all within approximately a 10 year time span: Meritaten, Meketaten, Ankhesenpaaten (also known as Ankhesenamen, the wife of Tutankhamen, her half-brother), Neferneferuaten-Tasherit, Neferneferure, and Setepenre. Nefertiti never bore Akhenaten any sons. Akhenaten's only known son was Tutankhamen, who is now believed, through DNA analysis, to have been the son of a full brother and sister. This means that Tutankhamen was not the child of Akhenaten's other well-known wife, lady Kiya, as had been thought for many years, but that he was the child of Akhenaten and one of Akhenaten's sisters. Akhenaten had at least four sisters, any of which could technically have mothered the child, but there is no evidence that would indicate which sister may have been Tutankhamen's mother. As is evidenced by Tutankhamen subsequent reign, Nefertiti's lack of sons was not much of an issue when it came to succession; Egyptian kings had frequently chosen an adoptive heir, usually one from the king's harem. Within the 18th Dynasty alone, Thutmose I was an adoptive heir, a general in the army with no close relation to Amenhotep I, and Thutmose II and Thutmose III were both the sons of minor wives.

Whilst the lack of a son was not a disaster for the succession, it may have reflected poorly upon Nefertiti's status. She already was unable to claim the status of being a "King's Daughter", and now she was denied the possibility of being a "King's Mother", meaning her influence would only last as long as she retained her status as "Great Wife of the King" beside her husband. As it turned out, her inability to bear a son did not end up diminishing her influence, as she continued to maintain a favored status alongside her husband and may even have held power in her own right after her husband's death.

Akhenaten and Nefertiti's first years of marriage, and their first years as king and queen of Egypt, were spent in Thebes, which ha dlong been the capital during the 18th Dynasty. One of the first possible records of Nefertiti comes from a private tomb in Thebes. In TT188, the tomb of the royal butler Parennefer, a lady accompanies the king as he worships the Aten. The lady depicted in the scene was not named, but it is highly probable that she was Nefertiti; throughout their years together Nefertiti and Akhenaten would be frequently depicted side by side in their worship and adoration of the god Aten.

Depiction of Nefertiti offering image of the goddess Maat to the Aten

Depiction of Nefertiti offering oil to the Aten

Like Queen Tiy, Nefertiti was depicted repeatedly alongside her husband and may have even featured more prominently than he in scenes on the temple walls of not only the Temple of Aten at Akhetaten but also at Karnak. Although their monuments and images were destroyed by later rulers, the surviving pieces of talatat (the small building blocks used to construct the temples and monuments of the Amarna period) that have been catalogued from both Karnak and Amarna indicate that Nefertiti was the prevailing figure in many scenes.

A talatat of Nefertiti and Akhenaten worshipping the Aten

A talatat depicting Nefertiti in worship to the Aten
It did not take long for Nefertiti to rise to a position of great prominence, far surpassing that of Tiy. The following is a list of the titles that Nefertiti held:

iryt-p't: Hereditary Princess
wrt-hzwt: Great of Praises
nbt-im3t: Lady of Grace
bnrt-mrwt: Sweet of Love
nbt-t3wy: Lady of the Two Lands
hmt-niswt-wrt-meryt.f: Chief Wife of the King, His Beloved
hmt-niswt-wrt-meryt.f: Great King's Wife, His Beloved
hnwt-hmwt-nbwt: Lady of all Women
hnwt-Shm'w-mhw: Mistress of Upper and Lower Egypt
Nfr nfrwitn Nfr.tjy.tj: Beauty of Aten, The Beautiful One has Come

Most of the titles bear a resemblance to those of previous queens, and to Tiy, such as Great King's Wife and Hereditary Princess. Others are more akin to the king's titles, like "Lady of the Two Lands" and "Mistress of Upper and Lower Egypt", but they are only indicative of her position as queen and nothing more. The title Hereditary Princess is a reference to the previous queen Ahmose-Nefertari, who was the daughter of the 17th Dynasty ruler Seqenenre Tao II and queen Ahotep I, and the granddaughter of queen Tetisheri and King Sekankhtenre Ahmose Tao I. She was also the mother of Amenhotep I and the great wife of her brother, king Ahmose I, the first ruler of the 18th Dynasty. Her titles included "King's Mother", "Great King's Wife", "God's Wife", "King's Daughter", "King's Sister", and "Hereditary Princess". It was Ahmose I who bestowed upon Ahmose-Nefertari the office of *Second Prophet of Amen* and the lands, goods, and administrators that went with it, and she was also made God's Wife of Amen. The endowment was placed not only upon her but upon her descendants as well, meaning the title of "Hereditary Princess" is an indication that Nefertiti may have been a descendant of Ahmose-

Nefertari. However, there is little evidence other than her possible parentage by Ay to connect her to the family line of Ahmose-Nefertari.

Despite the title of "Hereditary Princess", there is no apparent connection between Nefertiti and Amen or the position of God's Wife of Amen. However, this may be due to the pre-eminence that was given to the solar god Aten over that of all other gods early on in Akhenaten's reign. Akhenaten is most famously known for the changes he brought about to Egypt's religious practices during his reign, actions that would later earn him the title of "Heretic King" by historians. During the first year of the reign of Amenhotep IV, there was little indication of the changes that would take place in subsequent years. Amenhotep IV continued in his father's stead in a very conventional manner by initially completing building projects started by Amenhotep III, and he was depicted in traditional roles of kingship. For example, Pylon III at Karnak shows Amenhotep IV in the very traditional role of the king smiting Egypt's enemies. However, even in these traditional scenes, hints of what would come could be seen in how the god Re-Horakty dominates the scenes, and that Ra-Horakty been newly designated as "he who rejoices in the horizon his name 'Sunlight that is in the Disk'".

Limestone relief depicting Nefertiti in the kingly role of smiting a prisoner

When Amenhotep IV began his reign, he made sure to continue his father's building works, and to further the theological shift that placed evermore focus upon the sun-god, in particular that of Ra-Horakty. Ra-Horakty was traditionally represented as a falcon headed man, but as Amenhotep IV placed greater and greater emphasis upon the solar aspects of the god, Ra-Harakty became known as Aten. The sun disk had already become familiar imagery in association with Amenhotep III, so it did not take long for Amenhotep IV to introduce a completely new divine image and for the image of the falcon headed man to become the non-anthropomorphic sun disk with rays of light streaming out from it ending in hands. Thus Aten replaced Ra-Horakty, and cults made their final shift from the dominance of the god Amun to that of the god Aten, who was the creator now.

This final shift may have taken place during years 2-5 of Akhenaten's reign. During year 2 there was the unusual occurrence of Akhenaten's first *heb-sed* festival. This was a rather remarkable occasion due to *heb-sed* festivals traditionally being celebrated to display the king's continued virility and to confirm his ability to continue ruling. The festivals were most often held after 30 years on the throne, and every subsequent 30 years. Amenhotep III celebrated three *heb-seds* in year 30, 34, and 37. Still, it was not unheard of for a king to bend tradition to meet his own purposes, and a *heb-sed* festival was a time of celebration and revelry for all people and could thus be used to celebrate some other event in the monarch's life, or as a political tool to appease the populace. In the case of Akhenaten, the purpose of such an early *heb-sed* may have been intended to mark the changes that were about to happen with the emergence of the Aten as the dominant deity. It may have also just as easily been intended as a royal celebration of something such as a birthday, or it may have been meant to appease the general public. Whatever the purpose behind the festival, it was an odd occurrence.

After forming the identity of the god Aten, and Aten's new place in Egyptian theology as the "Grand Creator", Amenhotep IV strove to establish the new cult of the Aten in the traditional religious centers of Ancient Egypt, including that of Thebes. He even built a large temple complex to Aten in the main temple precinct of Thebes, but he met with little success, as the cult of Amun-Ra was still too strong there. Thus, Amenhotep IV decided to take more drastic measures, including disbanding the priesthoods of all the gods except that of Aten and re-diverting the funds from those cults to that of Aten. On top of that, he created a new religious center, and thus was the city of Akhetaten born. Akhetaten (Horizen of Aten) is located in middle Egypt in the al-Minya district, and it is known today as Amarna.

Despite this change in Egyptian theology, and the seeming hatred directed towards Akhenaten by his successors, no such discontent was apparent during his reign. This may have been because his religious "revolution" did not force a complete change in the religious, social, and administrative norms of Ancient Egypt. Many traditions and ideologies were continued or transformed into something new. Other cities still continued on as they had, and it was only at Amarna that the Aten was the sole deity. While the choice to break from Thebes to Akhetaten was a seemingly drastic one, it was not the first time a king of Egypt had moved the capital city; it was merely the first time a king intentionally built a new capital city.

The new city of Akhetaten was built very quickly, allowing for the royal court to establish residence there in year 5 of Amenhotep IV's reign. It was also around this time that he made the change from Amenhotep to Akhenaten, which roughly translates to "beneficial of the Aten" or "servant of the Aten".

Temple of the Aten in Akhetaten

The city of Akhetaten was first explored by the Prussian Exploration Expedition of 1842-1845. It was a unique find, in that no other such Ancient Egyptian town had ever been found. Its unusual history and short occupation allowed it to help survive the ravages of time, leaving behind a shell of what once had been. Its occupation only lasted through the reign of its creator which has greatly skewed the evidence found

The city had a linear layout with the more important buildings lying to either side of the "Royal Road", which ran north to south through the city. At the top of this avenue was the North palace, where the royal family resided, and along the road was the Great Temple of Aten. The seclusion of other cult chapels or temples was a direct reflection of the dominance of the Aten cult, and the theological changes brought about by Akhenaten.

At the southern end of the avenue was the South palace, which was an administration center. The town would have been somewhat unusual with only one religious cult, instead of at least a few other small temples or shrines to other gods. The class structure would be somewhat out of proportion as well, with the whole of the royal court, administrators, and skilled craftsmen making up a large portion of the population.

While Amarna was undoubtedly the new religious center of Egypt, it is not clear what its administrative duties were. Memphis had long since been the administrative capital of Ancient Egypt, and while one of Akhenaten's viziers was stationed at Amarna, the other remained in Memphis, which implies that Memphis was still functioning as an administrative center. During the Saite Period, the reigns of the 26th dynasty kings offer a possible parallel. They set up their capital in the city of Sias, but Memphis remained an administrative center. Memphis did not lose its position as such until the advent of Alexander the Great, and his creation of the city of

Alexandria, which soon became the religious, cultural, and political center of the country. So while administrative duties where probably seen to at Akhetaten, the administration of the whole of Egypt was still being overseen from Memphis.

Amarna was a city that was purposely built for its ruler to focus attention on the worship of the god Aten, but it was not a city that grew and developed over time. While the remains found in the city provide valuable insights into the Amaran Period, they are not as helpful in informing historians about the nature of the normal Egyptian town's layout, residents, and quality of life. During this Amarna period, the period in which Egypt's capital was situated at Akhetaten, much of what is known about life at that time comes from three main sources. The first source is art, including stelae, non-royal tombs, royal tombs, sculptures, etc. The second source is a set of documents, known as the Amarna tablets, and the third source is archaeological data.

Much of the art was found in the tombs near the city, which contained the remains of Akhetaten's elite inhabitants. The art includes multiple depictions of life in Akhetaten, like scenes of the king racing chariots from the North royal palace down to the southern administration palace. Other scenes depict the king and queen rewarding and appointing officials not from a throne room but from a balcony of the Southern palace. In other depictions the temple of Aten is a feature. Small shrines from private homes could be found with images of the royal family, including one that shows Amenhotep IV and Nefertiti playing with their young daughters. Judging from the young daughters' appearances in family scenes, of which there were many, many items are dated based on the number of daughters depicted in the art. For example, before Nefertiti and Akhenaten made the move to Amarna they had at least three of their six daughters; Meritaten, Meketaten, and Ankesenpaaten. Meanwhile, the couple's younger daughters, Neferneferiaten-Tasherit, Neferneferure, and Setepenre, appear in scenes at Akhetaten but not at Thebes.

Limestone reliefs depicting Akhenaten, Nefertiti and three of their daughters with the

Aten represented as beams of light.

The royal family, including the young princess, was always a central feature of Amarna art. One of Ancient Egypt's most highly acclaimed pieces of art, that of the dauntingly beautiful bust of Nefertiti (which now resides in a Berlin museum), came from Akhetaten. The art clearly demonstrates the revolutionary changes that occurred during the period. No longer is the king depicted as being strong, lithe and powerful; instead the rulers are depicted with a long drooping face, a rounded swollen belly, and curved thighs, features that are more akin to the female form and representations of fertility than that of an Egyptian king. Nefertiti is also depicted in this fecund style, giving credence to the theory that these changes were simply the result of artistic derivation, with a new theology, and a new city, came a new artistic style. A further representation of the creator/fertility aspect of the god Aten may be seen in the importance placed upon depictions of the whole royal family, king, queen, and princesses alike. No longer along the walls of the temples and those of the palaces did the images depicted follow a strict canon of set proportions. Instead, the images began to take on a more three dimensional quality, making them appear more fluid and lifelike. All of these changes are thought to represent the androgynous aspect of the Aten, to show him as cosmic creator, and the fertile giver of life, containing within himself both the male and the female aspects of divinity.

A talatat depicting Nefertiti

A further representation of this aspect of the god may be seen in the importance placed upon depictions of the whole royal family, including the king, queen, and princesses alike. Although not unheard of, it was uncommon for royal children to be depicted alongside their parents in official representations, but many such images are found at Amarna. Along the walls of the temples and those of the palaces the images depicted would have followed a strict canon of set proportions.

While the art of Amarna gives a window to glimpse through and see what life may have been like at Akhetaten, there are other sources of information that must be considered. The Amarna tablets may never be as awe-inspiring as Amarna art or the magnificent objects that were revealed in Tutankhamen's tomb, but they are historically indispensable. The tablets were found in 1888 by some local villagers who were digging at Amarna for marl when they came upon a number of crumbling wooden chests that held within them many clay tablets covered in writing on both sides. The antiquities authorities soon heard of the find and were able to collect together most of the tablets before they could be sold off on the antiquities market. Since then more fragments have been found by excavators and scholars.

What was most striking about these tablets was that despite having been found in chests whose lids bore the names of Amenhotep III and Amenhotep IV they were inscribed upon in Akkadian cuneiform. It soon became clear that the tablets formed part of a state administrative archive. The archive mostly consists of correspondence between the rulers, and diplomats of the Middle Eastern nations, including those of Babylonia, Assyria, Hitti, Mitanni, Syria, Canaan, and Ancient Egypt during the reigns of Amenhotep III and Akhenaten. They have become a primary source to historians for establishing the timeline of the early New Kingdom period of Ancient Egypt, and of gaining a greater understanding of the international diplomatic and administrative framework of the period. During the New Kingdom, Egypt established strong ties with its foreign neighbours, ties which Tutankhamen's widowed queen Ankhsenamun would try to call upon after his death.

It is from the Amarna letters that assumptions have been made concerning queen Tiy's influence over state affairs and over her son. She appears occasionally in the correspondence, yet Nefertiti never appears. This may be due to the one-sided nature of the letters, the gaps found within them or a lack of interest in foreign affairs by Akhenaten. While Nefertiti's religious duties are clearly and prominently depicted, little is known about her administrative duties. Queen Tiy was believed to have held great influence over state and foreign administration, as may be evidenced by the following letter written to her after the death of Amenhotep III and at the beginning of Amenhotep IV reign:

"Say to Tiy, the mistress of Egypt from Tushratta, King of Mitanni:

> With me all goes well. With you may all go well. With your household and your son, may all go well...You are the know who knows that I always showed love to Nimmuaria, your husband, and that Nimmuaria, your husband, always showed love to me...You are the one who knows much better than all others the things that we said to one another. No other person knows them as well as you... I will not forget my love for Nimmuaria, your husband. More than ever,

I now show this love tenfold for your son, Napkhururiya...I had asked your husband for statues of solid gold...But now Napkhururiya, your son, has sent plated statues of wood. With gold being as dirt in your son's land, why has your son not given what I asked for?...

It is clear that Tushratta felt that Tiy held influence over her son, and over administrative matters, but to what extent? It has been speculated that this may not have been a matter of political influence or power so much as simply one friend requesting the help of another, expecting no more than a mother's influence of her son. Amenhotep III kept diplomatic ties between vassal states strong, something that his son Akhenaten showed little need to do. Despite the lack of documentation and information, Nefertiti is still believed to have retained extensive influence within the royal court.

Fragmented relief depicting Nefertiti

There is little doubt that Nefertiti was a loving and caring mother, or that she and her daughters were loved by their father. The Ancient Egyptians, unlike their contemporaries, had always valued daughters along with sons. While a son may have brought more distinction to a mother or to a family, daughters were not discarded or viewed as being subsidiary. Although not unheard of, it was uncommon for royal children to be depicted alongside their parents in official representations, yet many such images are found at Amarna. In fact, throughout the 18th Dynasty there are multiple representations of royal princesses but very few of sons, and it remains unclear why sons are excluded from scenes. Of course, in the case of Nefertiti and Akhenaten, the exclusion of sons was most likely a simple case of there being no sons shared by the couple. Given the importance that was placed upon the family unit, it is unlikely that a son would have been excluded if he had existed.

Akhenaten's reign lasted from 1352-1336 B.C., and upon his death it is believed that he was buried not in the Valley of the Kings, which was the established burial area for the New Kingdom rulers, but in a royal tomb that was found outside of Akhetaten. Very little remains of the tomb, which suffered extensive damage in antiquity, but scattered remains of Akhenaten's sarcophagi indicate that he was most likely buried there.

It is around the time of Akhenaten's death that Nefertiti fades from the historical record; in fact she actually disappears from the historical record just after the death of her daughter Meritaten around year 12 of Akhenaten's reign. While that could suggest she died around that time, the lack of any evidence concerning a burial or any scenes of mourning have led historians to believe that she was still alive and well when Akhenaten passed.

What is known is that the famous pharaoh Tutankhamen succeeded Akhenaten eventually, but the transition of power from Akhenaten to Tutankhamen is full of controversy. Before Tutankhamen on the reignal lists, there are two other possible pharaohs named Smenkhare and Neferneferuaten. It is not known whether Smenkhare or Neferneferuaten ruled independently or if they were both co-regents with Akhenaten at some point. It has even been argued that they are one and the same person, though there is a general consensus that due to the feminine "t" ending found in Neferneferuaten's name that she was a female ruler. Smenkhare has a masculine name and is often depicted with another female by his side, presumably his wife, which makes it highly unlikely that the two rulers where the same person.

It has been suggested that Nefertiti may have held a co-regency with Akhenaten, particularly in light of some of her more kingly titles, which would make it more likely that she ruled on her own at some point after her husband's death. With that in mind, it is thought by some historians that Neferneferuaten was Nefertiti, although there is very little evidence to support this short of Nefertiti having been known to use the title herself. Inscriptions of the name Neferneferuaten in conjunction with Nefertiti were only ever found together with that of Akhenaten, and while it is possible that she ruled as co-regent with him, or even briefly on her own for a very short period after his death, there is no real evidence other than conjecture to support such a hypothesis. Evidence from the time around and just after Akhenaten's death is very fragmented and difficult to interpret. The only clear successive ruler indicated was Tutankhamen.

Even less is known about Smenkhare, who may have been the younger brother of Akhenaten (though there is no evidence that proves such a familial connection). There is very little evidence connecting Smenkhare to Nefertiti, other than the complete lack of conflicting evidence, and it is not known whether he ruled as co-regent before Neferneferuaten or after, or if he ruled independently for a time. The main documented reference to him as pharaoh comes from the tomb of Meryre II, in the Northern tomb necropolis at Amarna. While the actual scene is lost, it is recorded that there was a scene depicting the king Smenkhare and his great wife Meritaten handing out tribute from a balcony or "window of appearance", just as Akhenaten and Nefertiti were depicted doing. With the scene now being lost, it is difficult to determine Smenkhare's place within the royal 18ᵗʰ dynasty line. Very little is known about the end of Akhenaten's reign, and the possible rule of Smenkhare and/or Neferneferuaten. It is not until the reign of Tutankhamen that the historical record becomes clearer again.

As a result, the lack of information concerning the end of Akhenaten's reign means there's a lack of information surrounding the rest of Nefertiti's life.

Chapter 5: Nefertiti's Death and Burial

A granite statue of Nefertiti's head carved in a way that allows different hairstyles to adorn the head

The question of Nefertiti's status after the death of Akhenaten is further confused by the fact that all mention of her seems to disappear, so nothing is known about her death. It is not known when she died, how she died, or where she died, and her body has never been positively identified. The reason for Nefertiti's disappearance from the historical record is unclear, but it did coincide with death of her daughter Meritaten. A plague swept through the region during this period, and Meritaten is thought to have died from the illness, leading some to hypothesize that Nefertiti also died around the same time. However, given the extensive scenes of mourning by both parents found in Akhenaten's tomb for Meritaten, and the complete lack of any mourning scenes of Nefertiti, this theory is full of holes. And if Nefertiti had died in year 12 of her husband's reign, it seems logical that she would have been interred in Akhenaten's tombs and that his grief over her passing would have been great, and worthy of depiction.

It is more likely that Nefertiti survived Akhenaten, and her disappearance from the historical record suggests nothing other than the fact that historians lack all of the documents of the period. Either way, what happened to her after his death can only be guessed at. Moreover, her mummy has yet to be positively identified. There is only a small broken shabti figure, with an inscription referring to Nefertiti, that connects her to Akhenaten's tomb and burial, and it remains the only evidence regarding her own burial. The Shabti figurine reads, "The Heiress high and mighty in the palace, one trusted of the King of Upper and Lower Egypt Neferkheperure Waenre, the son of Re (Akhenaten), Great in his lifetime, the Chief Wife of the King, Neferneferuaten-Nefertiti, Living forever and ever."

At the beginning of the 21st century, some believed that the "Elder Lady" mummy might be Nefertiti, based on its location and the age of the mummy, which was in her 30s-40s. Busts of Nefertiti suggested some resemblance with the mummy as well. However, DNA analysis and other examinations conclusively proved that the "Elder Lady" mummy was the daughter of Yuya and Thuya, thus eliminating Nefertiti and seemingly verifying that it was Queen Tiy.

With the "Elder Lady" ruled out, speculation has turned to one of the unidentified mummies found alongside the Elder Lady mummy in tomb KV35 in the Valley of the Kings. The mummy has been nicknamed "The Younger Lady", and some Egyptologists have argued that it is Nefertiti herself based on descriptions of the mummy as being a 5'2 woman around the age of 25. Substantial damage had been done to the mummy, likely by grave robbers during antiquity, but the woman had suffered a fatal wound to her jaw area. Other evidence, including the mummification techniques and the use of embalming fluid, all suggested it was an 18th Dynasty mummy, which makes sense since it was buried next to Queen Tiy. Those insisting the Younger Lady mummy is Nefertiti also argue that beads and a rare wig found in the tomb lend credence to their theory.

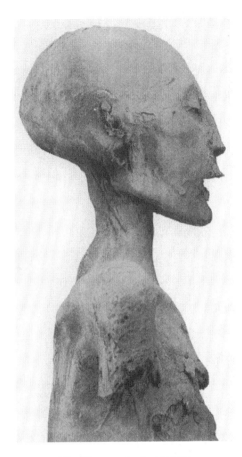

The Younger Lady mummy

However, most Egyptologists dismiss the theory, or at least continue to insist that there's no way to conclusively prove the mummy is Nefertiti. One sticking point among them is that no DNA analysis could prove Nefertiti's identity because it remains unclear who her parents were, and the remains of her children have never been positively identified either. One recent study analyzed the mummy and came to the conclusion that the Younger Lady may have been Tutankhamen's mother or one of Amenhotep III's daughters, while others have even thrown out the possibility that the mummy is Meritaten, the daughter of Nefertiti and Akhenaten who may have died of plague near the 12th year of his reign. On top of all that, the search for Nefertiti is further complicated by the fact that Tutankhamen reversed some of his father's theological changes and is believed to have eventually had his relatives moved from Akhetaten and reinterred in the Valley of Kings. Whatever the case, without being able to identify the mummy with certainty, it could be one of the dozens of royal wives or daughters who lived during the 18th Dynasty, a period of time spanning more than two centuries.

Due to the lack of a body, and burial for Nefertiti, any conclusions concerning her death remain pure speculation. Perhaps that has helped her maintain a special place among contemporary societies across the world. With interest in Ancient Egypt as high as ever, Nefertiti remains an enigmatic queen, and all that is known for sure about her is that she was the Great Wife of one of Egypt's most notorious rulers, Amenhotep IV/Akhenaten, that she bore him at least 6 daughters, and that she shared a position of near equality with her husband religiously if not politically.

Bibliography

Aldred, Cyril, 1988, *Akhenaten, King of Egypt*, London.

Davies, N., 1923, 'Akhenaten at Thebes', *JEA 9*, 136-145.

Dodson, Aidan, 2009, *Amarna Sunset,* New York.

Hornung, Erik, 1999, *Akhenaten and the Religion of Light*, London.

Redford, D.B., 1984, *Akhenaten: The Heretic King*, Princeton.

Tyldesley, Joyce, 1998, *Nefertiti*, New York.

Cleopatra

Cleopatra, as shown in a contemporary bust.

Chapter 1: The Woman Ruler

In 1963, the world was fascinated by the sudden, whirlwind romance of two of its biggest film stars, Elizabeth Taylor and Richard Burton, who despite the fact that they were both married, had begun a torrid love affair. The two had met, and fallen for each other, during the filming of the Hollywood epic *Cleopatra*, with Liz Taylor in the titular role and Burton as – who else? – the gallant Roman general Mark Antony. It is a testament to what is, along with the likes of Lancelot and Guinevere and Romeo and Giuliet, one of the world's best known love stories – and all the more remarkable because it is, for the most part, true.

Yet Cleopatra's romance with Mark Antony was just the culmination of a life that was, in a great many aspects, truly remarkable in its own right. Throughout the ages she has been cast in every part: from being reviled as the personification of evil feminine wiles doing their work over great men, all the way to iconic heroine of the feminist movement. Sometimes, she has depicted as the most beautiful woman of her age, on other occasions she has been described as plain. Academics and laypeople have argued strenuously over whether she was a hopeless romantic, doomed to fall for great and charismatic men, or a ruthless politician bent on using her charms to seduce the world's most powerful figures and bend them to her will. Even her physical appearance is something of a mystery, with depictions in Greco-Roman art differing wildly from those which appear in art produced in Egypt around the time of her life and reign. Yet for all the mystery surrounding her – or perhaps because of it – Cleopatra continues to captivate popular imagination to this day, and remains one of the most iconic female rulers of all time.

Cleopatra, or as she was formally known, Cleopatra VII Thea Philopator (Cleopatra VII, Goddess, Father-Lover) was born in Alexandria in 69 BC. Her father was the Pharaoh Ptolemy XII Auletes, but because of the incestuous nature of royal marriages in Egypt, it is unclear who her mother was – it appears likely that she was another Cleopatra, Cleopatra V. Like all the Ptolemies, Cleopatra was not Egyptian. Tracing her ancestry back far enough – and indeed, not even that far – demonstrates Cleopatra was descended from minor Macedonian landed nobility and was, in effect, a full-blooded Greek without a drop of Egyptian blood in her. The dynasty to which she belonged had been established by Ptolemy, who took the name Ptolemy I Soter (Savior), a Macedonian general who had been a close childhood friend and then campaign companion to Alexander the Great. Alexander had conquered Egypt while destroying the mighty Persian empire some three centuries before, and after his death, when the wars of the *Diadochii* (the Successors) tore his empire asunder, it was Ptolemy who came to take over Egypt and establish himself there as a ruler. Ptolemy's dynasty had endured ever since, molded in the image of the old Pharaohs that the Persian Empire had long since crushed.

The Ptolemaic dynasty, like the Pharaohs of old, had a tendency to pursue incestuous inter-marriage between brother and sister, though this seems not to have affected Cleopatra in any way – all contemporary sources, whether they disliked her or not, unanimously agree that she was neither deformed or feeble-minded. However, though she suffered no disadvantages due to her birth, the environment she grew up in was hardly the most harmonious for a child. The court of the latter Ptolemies was a veritable snake's nest of plots, deceit, murder and corruption, and never more so than under the reign of the unfortunate Ptolemy XII Auletes, Cleopatra's father. Ptolemy XII's accession to the throne was marked by plotting and bribery on a grand scale, and once he was in place he grew so paranoid that, suspicious of his provincial governors, he insisted on concentrating almost all executive powers in Alexandria, where he had his seat. Such a system of government could not hope to cope with, or indeed understand, the problems faced by the Egyptian kingdom's most farspread provinces, and inevitably there were violent uprisings by those subjects at the borders of the kingdom who felt themselves abandoned to their fate. Cyprus and Cyrenaica were both lost, and other rebellions were crushed only with great difficulty and expense. At this time, Egypt had effectively become a client state of Rome – and a valued trading asset, as they provided the majority of grain imports to the capital – and, in 58 BC, despite unrest at home, Ptolemy was obliged to travel to Rome on an official visit. He chose to take Cleopatra, then just a child, with him as well, but what was meant to be a short trip ended up becoming a three-year exile: taking advantage of his absence, another Cleopatra seized the throne. It is, unfortunately, unclear which Cleopatra this was, exactly. Records from the period are sparse and not helped by the fact that the Ptolemies favored re-using the same names over and over again. She may either have been Cleopatra V, making her Cleopatra VII's mother, or Cleopatra VI, which would mean she was a sister. Either way, this Cleopatra's reign was to be short-lived – within a few months of her accession to the throne, she died suddenly under mysterious circumstances. It is highly likely that she was murdered, most probably at the hand of Berenice IV, Cleopatra VII's older sister, who took the throne as soon as she died. Berenice reigned for just under three years in Alexandria, until Ptolemy XII finally returned, at the head of a Roman army led by General Aulus Gabinius. Ptolemy had been forced to go hat in hand to Rome, having virtually no support outside of Alexandria and no chance of regaining his throne by raising armies of his own. Though this move allowed Ptolemy to recapture the throne of Egypt, he had effectively made his kingdom a vassal state of Rome, garrisoned by Roman armies, propped up by Roman spears, and dependent on Roman goodwill.

Betrayed by at least one of his eldest daughters, if not two (or his wife), Ptolemy seems to have turned to Cleopatra, his companion during his three-year exile, as his sole repository of trust. At age 14, he proclaimed her regent, a largely ceremonial position which nonetheless placed her in direct line to the throne in the event of his death. Ptolemy's reign limped on for another four years, amid further losses of crucial territory and an ever-growing dependence on Gabinius's troops, whose officers had established themselves – apparently permanently – in Egypt and promptly formed their own political faction, the *Gabiniani*, in order to try and carve themselves their own piece of the rich Egyptian pie. Finally, in 51 BC, Ptolemy Auletes died, leaving an 18-year-old Cleopatra at a nonplus. She could not assume sole rulership, for such an act would require her to get rid of her younger brother, Ptolemy XIII, with whom she was expected to share power. Cleopatra was also, in keeping with dynastic tradition, required to marry Ptolemy, who was 10 years old at the time. With the weight of tradition upon her, Cleopatra complied, but her and Ptolemy's was not a happy union. The two seem not to have gotten along as brother and sister, never mind as husband and wife, and matters were not made any easier by the fact that the gods themselves seemed to be conspiring against Cleopatra. Her rule was marked by more uprisings, and to add insult to injury, the Nile stubbornly refused to deliver adequate floods. Egypt's fertile grain fields were dependent on the periodic flooding of the Nile basin, which would coat the fields with a natural fertiliser, but a sparse flood meant even sparser harvests, which meant not only that the people would go hungry but that Egypt would be unable to deliver sufficient grain to Rome, with all the perilous consequences that entailed.

Feeling the strain, just a few months after ascending to the throne, Cleopatra effectively divorced her younger brother, whose influence was limited by reason of his age – she no longer appeared with him at official ceremonies, and started being the sole signatory on official documents, a gross breach of tradition. In Ptolemaic tradition, female co-rulers were technically subordinate to their male counterparts, regardless of whether this was actually the case, so doing away with Ptolemy was a slap in the face to the many traditionalists at court. Cleopatra may have been many things, but she was never anything but brash – perhaps even foolish. Having made enemies of the traditionalists, she promptly followed this political *faux pas* in 50 BC by upsetting one of the most powerful political factions in Egypt, the *Gabiniani*. Having been in Egypt, at a loose end, for approximately five years, the *Gabiniani* had essentially severed their ties to Rome, becoming embroiled in the civil war currently wracking the fledgling Empire in their own right.

When some exponents of the *Gabiniani* murdered the sons of Marcus Bibulus, the governor of Syria, who had been sent in friendship to request their aid in a military campaign against the neighbouring Parthians, Cleopatra saw a chance to intervene and cut the *Gabiniani* down to size. She had the assassins seized, put in chains, and delivered to Bibulus, but while this may have curried favour with the Roman governor, it did nothing to endear her to the *Gabiniani*, who promptly went from uneasy allies to sworn enemies. Cleopatra could hardly hope to rule long in the face of such massed political hostility, and in 48 BC, a plot spearheaded by Pothinus, a eunuch in the palace service, with the collusion of Cleopatra's many enemies, forced her from the throne and placed the more biddable, pliant Ptolemy XIII on it as sole ruler of Egypt. Cleopatra was a fugitive.

Chapter 2: Two Civil Wars in One

Cleopatra Appears before Caesar, by Leon Jerome
Cleopatra did not take her exile lying down. She immediately attempted to raise the province

of Persilium against her brother, but faced with lack of support, she was forced to flee deep into the interior. Ptolemy sent troops to apprehend her, but the teenaged ruler had other, bigger fish to fry.

Rome, Egypt's *de facto* overlord, was in the process of tearing herself apart, and the repercussions of this conflict were being felt across the Mediterranean. Gaius Julius Caesar, former consul and governor of Gaul, had marched across the Rubicon, illegally bringing his armies onto Italian soil and threatening Rome herself, with the purpose of making himself dictator. Caesar was opposed by his former ally, the once-great general Pompey Magnus, but Pompey was an old, spent man while Caesar was still vigorous, and Caesar had chased Pompey's army from Rome, hounded it all the way to southern Italy, and then, when Pompey escaped across the Mediterranean to Greece, he had loaded his army onto a fleet and shipped it across the sea, where he had annihilated Pompey's armies at Pharsalus in 48 BC. Pompey had barely escaped with his life, and virtually alone and penniless, he had taken ship for Egypt, where he arrived as a supplicant, possibly hoping for military assistance from the *Gabiniani*, or from Ptolemy himself.

Having heard a rumor that Pompey was attempting to raise men against him in Egypt, Caesar took ship for Alexandria, only to find upon his arrival that Pompey had been murdered on the orders of Egypt's young pharaoh, the boy-king Ptolemy XIII. Possibly encouraged by Pothinus, Ptolemy had Pompey Magnus put to death almost immediately after his arrival in Egypt, the end result apparently being that he hoped to ingratiate himself with Caesar, whose victory at Pharsalus had, by default, made him the uncontested ruler of Rome and thus the most powerful man in the known world.

Bust of Pompey

Ptolemy, however, had completely, monumentally misunderstood Caesar. When the Roman general arrived in Egypt a bare two days later, hot on Pompey Magnus's heels, Ptolemy received Caesar with great pomp and presented him with Pompey's head. He could not have insulted Caesar more, or rendered him more furious, if he had slapped him in the face. Pompey had been a close friend of Caesar's before their rivalry spiralled out of control, and had even married Caesar's daughter, who had died in childbirth before the war.

Utterly enraged by what he referred to as Ptolemy's casual barbarism, Caesar asserted Rome's superiority over Egypt – not to mention the fact he had an army on Egyptian soil – by installing himself in Alexandria and proclaiming himself arbiter of the dispute between Cleopatra and Ptolemy. All of this quickly reached Cleopatra, who had plenty of spies in the Egyptian court, and she realised that Ptolemy's colossal blunder was a heaven-sent chance to reassert her claim to the Egyptian throne. Already fairly certain that Caesar's new-found loathing for Ptolemy would lead him to side with her in any case, Cleopatra decided to strike while the iron was hot. She quickly travelled to Alexandria, where Caesar had taken up residence in Ptolemy's palace. At a loss as to how to actually enter the palace itself, which was heavily patrolled by Ptolemy's personal guard in addition to Caesar's own men, she finally settled upon an idea which has fascinated the world ever since. She had one of her followers, Apollodorus the Sicilian, wrap her into a carpet, hoist her onto his shoulder, and march her past the palace guards.

When Apollodorus was received by Caesar, he unrolled the carpet and Cleopatra, slightly dishevelled but otherwise none the worse for wear, appeared before the Roman general. Caesar was 52 at the time, just over three decades older than Cleopatra, who was 21, but Cleopatra might well have known that Caesar was something of a womaniser, having already conducted a famous affair with Servilia, the mother of Marcus Brutus. Be that as it may, Cleopatra chose to appear before Caesar virtually *en desabilhee*, wearing little to nothing, and most of the sources from the ancient world agree that the Egyptian queen was a famous beauty. She seduced him, by all accounts, that very night, and it seems the ever ambitious Roman eventually came away impressed by the lavish and exotic lifestyles Egypt's royalty enjoyed.

It is unclear whether Cleopatra ever truly loved Caesar – that is something that only she can ever have truly known – but she was certainly canny enough to realise the political advantages of a liaison with him. Prior to Caesar and Cleopatra's meeting, all evidence pointed to Caesar intending to do away with Egyptian independence altogether, and formally annex Egypt into the Roman dominion. However, after they began their relationship in such a spectacular fashion, Caesar promptly discarded his annexation plans and became the principal backer of Cleopatra's claim to the throne of Egypt.

Ptolemy was not prepared to take Cleopatra's sudden ascendancy lying down, however. Shortly after Caesar made his formal announcement of support for Cleopatra's claim he fled the city with most of his entourage, and raised his armies. Caesar, who had only 4,000 men with him, could not hope to fight, so for almost a year between 48 and 47 BC he and Cleopatra were besieged inside a compound within Alexandria's walls. However, the besieging force was unable to breach the compound and seems to have contented itself with attempting to starve Caesar and Cleopatra out, something which was impossible as they were able to keep their lines of communication open and resupply themselves via fortified access to the sea, which the compound possessed. In January of 47 BC, Caesar managed to get word to Mithridates of Pergamum – an ancient rival of Egypt, ever since the wars of the *Diadochii* – and request his aid.

Mithridates marched with some 16,000 men, causing Ptolemy's forces to fall back. Caesar sallied from Alexandria, combined his forces with Mithridates, and marched upon Ptolemy's army.

The two armies, both around 20,000 strong, met at the Nile shortly afterwards. Caesar's veterans, the shock troops, were in the vanguard and they attacked the Egyptian troops, which were equipped as a traditional Macedonian Phalanx with heavy bronze armour, shields, and 18-foot pikes. Roman armament and tactics were superior to the Phalanx, something they had already amply proved in their conquest of Greece, and Caesar's men and their allies made short work of Ptolemy's force, instigating a rout. Ptolemy himself was caught in the headlong, panicked rush for safety, and he drowned attempting to cross the Nile. With his death, Cleopatra became *de facto* sole ruler of Egypt, with Caesar's blessing, though for formality's sake she married Ptolemy XIV, another brother, to appease the traditionalists at court. Caesar chose to linger in Alexandria for a further three months, despite his presence being urgently required in Rome. During this time, Cleopatra also gave birth to a boy, whom she named Ptolemy "Caesarion" Caesar, who she claimed to her dying day was Caesar's son, though Caesar himself steadfastly refused to formally acknowledge the boy as his.

Having ended the Egyptian civil war in Alexandria, Caesar was ready to return to Rome, which was about to be introduced to Egypt's young queen. At this point in his life, Caesar had been married to Calpurnia, who he had taken as a wife in 59 B.C., but having extramarital relationships was hardly abnormal for a powerful Roman at the time.The following year, in 46 BC, Cleopatra visited Caesar in Rome, where he was in the process of having himself proclaimed dictator for life, much to the chagrin of his opponents in the Senate. Her visit provoked something of a scandal; foreign mistresses were all very well, and it was accepted that a Roman general might warm his bed any which way he chose when he was away from home, and heads would be politely turned the other way. It was quite another matter, however, for Caesar to openly flaunt his mistress before all and sundry, and especially before his long-suffering wife, Calpurnia, who retired into seclusion over the matter.

Several of Caesar's enemies, most notably the famous orator Cicero, were outspoken in their disgust for Caesar's relationship with the Egyptian queen, but Caesar appears not to have cared – possibly as a consequence of his growing arrogance. He appeared publicly arm in arm with Cleopatra on a number of formal occasions, and commissioned a gold-lacquered statue of Cleopatra, depicting her as the Egyptian goddess Isis, to be placed in the temple of Venus Genetrix he had personally endowed. He was canny enough, however, not to give in to Cleopatra's repeated insistences that he make Caesarion his heir, something he could not theoretically do, in any case, since Cleopatra was not a Roman citizen. Cleopatra was desperate for her son to be proclaimed Caesar's successor, but in the event Caesar chose to appoint his nephew, Gaius Octavian, as his heir, with a provision that if Octavian should die before him then his inheritance should pass to Marcus Brutus, his former lover Servilia's son. In the next two years, Cleopatra was often in Rome, alternating her time between there and Alexandria which, thanks to Caesar's intervention and diplomacy, was finally stable enough to allow her to leave the city for months at a time. Most of the factions who had plotted against her had been crushed, and with no other pretenders to the throne and the biddable Ptolemy XIV as her co-ruler, Cleopatra was reasonably satisfied. Barring the matter of Caesarion's succession, she could not have been happier.

Cicero

The bliss was not to last. On the Ides of March in 44 BC, Caesar was murdered by a mob of Senators on the floor of the Senate House, victim of a plot orchestrated chiefly by his would-be-heir, Marcus Brutus. When Caesar entered the Senate House, he was approached, as arranged, by a *Liberator* named Tillius Cimber, who presented him with a petition for the cancellation of the exile of his brother, who had been banished some time previously. Caesar ignored him and brushed roughly past, but Cimber seized hold of his robe, half-pulling his toga from him. Caesar snatched his toga away from Cimber, demanding "What is this violence?". It was at this point that Servilius Casca, who despite his confession to Antony had decided to go along with the plot after all – doubtless in fear of what the other *Liberatores* would do to him if he got cold feet – attacked. He also seized Caesar by his robe and, drawing his dagger, dealt the Dictator a glancing cut to the neck. Casca was no assassin, and the cut seems to have been trivial, so much so that Caesar, who had doubtless seen worse on campaign, turned and seized him by the neck, snarling "What are you doing, you wretch?". Casca panicked and, dropping his dagger, screamed "Help me, brothers!". His desperate entreaty broke the paralysis that had seized his fellow *Liberatores*, with upwards of 60 men descending upon Caesar. The Senators were not military men, which was made clear by the haphazard manner in which they stabbed Caesar with knives and daggers. Caesar, stabbed multiple times, tripped and fell to the ground, where the conspirators continued to savage him. Despite the fact Caesar was stabbed nearly two dozen times, doctors concluded only one of them was a fatal wound.

It has been suggested that it was Servilia who, jealous of Cleopatra, planted the idea of a plot into her son's head, though it will never be possible to know the whole truth of the matter. Cleopatra, who was in Rome at the time, was forced to flee for her life. She took shelter in Alexandria, devastated by Caesar's death, and secluded herself in mourning.

Cleopatra, as shown in a contemporary Egyptian statue.

Chapter 3: Cleopatra and Antony

Following Caesar's death, aside from her desire for vengeance, Cleopatra's first instinct seems to have been to protect her son Caesarion, and ensure his future. Caesar had died without naming Caesarion heir, or indeed even formally recognising him as a son and Roman citizen, and his position in Egypt was also far from secure. As the well-publicized bastard of a Roman, he could not hope to inherit Cleopatra's crown, so Cleopatra had to act.

Just a few months after Caesar was brutally slain in the Senate House, Cleopatra quietly did away with Ptolemy XIV (it has never been proven that she was behind his sudden death, but family tradition suggests that when a Ptolemy becomes fatally indisposed, his closest relatives usually have a hand in the matter), and Cleopatra formally raised Caesarion to the title of co-regent and successor, since at that point there were no more male Ptolemies to take the throne in his stead. Having firmly established Caesarion as her heir, Cleopatra could turn her eye to foreign affairs: Rome was once again in the process of tearing herself apart, with Brutus and Cassius, the chief plotters involved in Caesar's death, on the one side, and Octavian (Caesar's heir) and Mark Antony, a veteran of Caesar's Gaulish, Italian and Greek campaigns and dashing hero of the Roman mob, on the other. There were two distinct factions vying for supremacy, as there had been when her brother Ptolemy had fatally made the choice that cost him his throne and his life – the question was, could Cleopatra choose any more wisely?

Antony

Cleopatra was faced with the first great crisis of her reign since Caesar had first disposed of Ptolemy XIII and placed her upon the throne, and she reacted with her customary impulsiveness, although her decision was almost certainly a foolish one. Brutus and Cassius, following an incident in the aftermath of Caesar's death when Mark Antony's oratory had incensed the Roman mob into howling for their blood, had fled Italy with the legions loyal to them and taken refuge in Asia Minor, where they had set about carving out a power-base for themselves, with remarkable success. Their position, so perilously close to Egyptian territory, meant that they directly threatened Cleopatra's throne, particularly as the ever-fickle Nile had once again delivered unsatisfactory floods, meaning that Egypt was wracked by famine, and the army severely weakened.

However, Cleopatra would never agree to ally herself with Egypt's enemies. Instead, she sent aid to Publius Dolabella, a prominent supporter of Caesar's who had aligned himself with Antony and Octavian and who also held a power-base in the East. Dolabella was hardly a match for Brutus and Cassius, though, and in 43 BC his forces were surrounded and destroyed, with Dolabella himself committing suicide to avoid capture and the dishonor of defeat, in the traditional patrician manner. Cassius was furious at Cleopatra's defiance, and realizing Egypt's extremely vulnerable position, he quickly outfitted an army with the intention of invading Egypt, removing her forcibly from the throne, and annexing her territory to the former conspirators' eastern domains. However, even as the expedition was about to set out in autumn of 43 BC, Cleopatra was – unwittingly – saved at the eleventh hour by Brutus, who recalled Cassius and his army to Smyrna, where he needed reinforcements against the forces of Antony and Octavian.

Brutus

Despite the recall, Cassius was not prepared to have Cleopatra's troops come to Antony and Octavian's aid, so he left one of his crack generals, Lucius Murcius, in command of a veteran legion and a fleet of approximately 60 ships, with which Murcius garrisoned a cape on the southern tip of Greece, knowing Cleopatra's fleet must pass nearby if she was to reinforce the Caesarians. Cleopatra, either because she was unaware of Murcius' ambush or because she trusted that she could defeat him, embarked her army onto her fleet and sailed nevertheless, but adverse weather proved to be her downfall. The Mediterranean is a treacherous sea to this day, especially in winter, and Cleopatra's fleet was smashed and scattered by a violent storm which lasted for days, causing Cleopatra herself, who had insisted on accompanying the expedition, to become violently sick. The remnants of her ships turned tail and limped back for Alexandria, while to the east, Murcius had to fight nothing but the wreckage of several of her galleys, which washed up on the shore he was patrolling.

Cleopatra's forces were fatally weakened, and she herself for a time was bedridden and too ill to attend to affairs of state. If Brutus and Cassius had been victorious, doubtless Egypt would have been made short work of. In the event, however, later in 42 BC, the armies of the two former conspirators were destroyed by Mark Antony and Octavian at Philippi, in Northen Greece. This victory effectively destroyed Brutus and Cassius, leaving Octavian, Antony and their ally Lepidus in control of Rome, having established Rome's second triumvirate (the first having been Caesar, Pompey, and Crassus).

Octavian was given Rome and the West, Lepidus Africa and Iberia, and Antony himself took the east as his personal domain. Accordingly, in 41 BC he summoned Cleopatra to his seat in Tarsus. It appears that Cleopatra had been accused of paying a massive bribe to Cassius to ensure the safeguarding of Egypt, which had allowed him to levy more troops and pay more mercenaries to oppose the Caesarians. Whether the accusations were true is a matter of debate, but either way Antony wanted to have words with Cleopatra personally, in order to test her loyalty. Another reason for the meeting was that Antony intended to wage war against the Parthians, Rome's age-old enemy in the East, and to do so he needed the logistic and financial support of Egypt. Perhaps he simply wanted to meet the famous beauty who had so completely seduced his old friend Caesar for himself.

Be it as it may, Cleopatra presented herself before him at Tarsus in the winter of 41 BC, arriving with all the pomp and circumstance that a queen of Egypt could summon. Like Caesar before him, Antony fell for her – or was seduced by her – almost on sight. Once again, it is unclear – as we will see from her later actions – whether Cleopatra truly loved Antony, or was just using him for his power. Perhaps the question is not so cut-and-dried, and she was doing a bit of both. Antony himself was so captivated by her that he chose to spend the remainder of the winter and the spring of 40 BC in Alexandria with her, exciting scandal in Rome not just as a consequence of their liaison – Cleopatra had been the mistress of Antony's closest friend, after all, and Antony had a wife, the Roman aristocrat Fulvia – but because, taking advantage of Antony's power in the east, Cleopatra had her sister Arsinoe murdered. Arsinoe, who was Cleopatra's one surviving sibling, was likely more than familiar enough with her other siblings' fates, and as the last one standing she had taken refuge at the temple of Artemis, in Ephesus (Greece), which was under Antony's jurisdiction. Arsinoe claimed the right of sanctuary, but that hardly stopped Antony's henchmen, who dragged her onto the temple steps and butchered her, thus removing once and for all the last credible threat to Cleopatra's throne. This elicited great scandal in Rome, where the right of sanctuary was held to be sacred, and Octavian, who was at odds with Antony, wasted no chance to use the story to discredit him.

A bust of Octavian, circa 30 B.C.

In late spring of 40 BC, Antony abruptly cut his relationship with Cleopatra short. Whether he feared the relationship would utterly condemn him in the eyes of the mob, or he felt guilty over the predicament of his wife Fulvia, who despite the rumors concerning him and Cleopatra's liaison – or possibly disbelieving them – was steadfastly campaigning on his behalf against Octavian, is unclear. What is certain, however, is that the relationship between Antony and Cleopatra, however brief, had been intense. Nine months later, Cleopatra gave birth to twins, Alexander Helios and Cleopatra Selene, who could only be Antony's children. Quite what

Cleopatra made of Antony's abandonment, however, is unclear. In all likelihood, she was fairly confident he would be back – he had a war against Parthia to prosecute, after all, for which Egypt would be an ideal base, and her seat in Alexandria was the wealthiest city in Antony's new domain.

Antony set out for Rome, but while he was on his way there he received news that his wife, Fulvia, had died prematurely while still steadfastly opposing Octavian's political smear campaign against him. Seeing a chance to patch things up with Octavian, Antony agreed he would remarry, to seal the alliance that would keep the crumbling triumvirate alive, at least for a time. Accordingly, later that year he married Octavian's own younger sister, Octavia Minor, as Pompey Magnus had once married Caesar's daughter, to preserve the unity of the first triumvirate. Cleopatra must have been less than thrilled at this union, especially as she was heavily pregnant with Antony's twins, to which she gave birth two months later, but Antony had his plate full ensuring support for his cause at home, and with the ever troublesome Parthians.

It was at this time that the Parthians, apparently sensing weakness, advanced eastwards, conquering large swathes of Syria and Judaea, which were essentially Antony's backyard. Capitalizing on the renewed goodwill engendered by his marriage with Octavia, Antony convinced his fellow triumvir Octavian to provide him with an army and sufficient supplies, and set off for Parthia to drive the enemy's forces from his domains and then, if all went well, to march into the Parthian heartland itself. However, Antony detoured to Greece on his way, where he scandalized Roman public opinion by proclaiming himself the incarnation of the god Dionysus, displaying a foreshadowing of the penchant for gluttony which would come to haunt his and Cleopatra's final days. Meanwhile, Octavian had re-routed the army he had promised Antony to Sicily, where a rebellion by one of Pompey Magnus's sons was underway. Despite attempts by Octavia to patch things up between her husband and her brother, in 38 BC Antony decided that Octavian would never truly support his Parthian venture and so, in disgust, he abandoned his wife and children in Rome and set sail for Alexandria.

It appears that Cleopatra took her erstwhile lover's return in stride, and there appears to be no doubt that the couple happily reunited. With her trademark impulsiveness, Cleopatra pledged Antony the money he needed to fund his Parthian expedition from the Egyptian royal treasury, and Antony married Cleopatra, according to Egyptian customs, later that year – Octavia's presence in Rome being conveniently forgotten. Antony then left Cleopatra behind and marched to war, achieving some notable initial successes in Judaea in 37 BC, where he installed Herod on the throne. He then marched on Parthia, but his campaign proved to be a catastrophe. A full quarter of his 100,000-man army was lost to disease, desertion and battle, and Antony was unsuccessful in subduing either Parthia or Armenia, being forced instead to limp back to Cleopatra with his tail between his legs.

While Antony struggled in the east, back in Rome Octavian had dismissed Lepidus, the third member of the Second Triumvirate, and assumed sole power over his domains, while also continuing a vigorous smear campaign against Antony, denouncing him for abandoning Octavia and his children and accusing him of having gone native with his wanton Egyptian queen.

Octavian's public relations offensive blamed Antony's recent failure and the consequent loss of Roman life on the wrath of the gods for Antony's sins.

Antony and Cleopatra, however, seem to have been unconcerned with Octavian's threats, or the growing popular resentment with Antony that Octavian was fomenting in Rome. It seems quite likely that Antony simply did not care any more and just wanted to be left alone in his Alexandrian idyll with the woman he loved. Like Caesar, Antony was fully charmed by the quixotic and exotic Egyptian lifestyle, and he immersed himself in it even more than his famous mentor. Despite repeated demands from Octavian that he return to Rome immediately to answer for his ill-conduct, Antony remained happily in Alexandria, and waged a new campaign against the Armenians in 34 BC, this time achieving success and annexing the territory to his and Cleopatra's domains.

It was in the aftermath of this war that Cleopatra and Antony finally overstepped their mark. Cleopatra organised a lavish, Roman-style Triumph in Alexandria to mark Antony's successful conquest, during which Antony's children (now numbering three) by Cleopatra were all granted royal titles in the East, Cleopatra herself was named Queen of Queens and ruler of the East, and crucially, Cleopatra's son Caesarion was named King of Kings, ruler of Egypt and the East, living God, and above all – Caesar's formal sole son and heir, thereby by default disowning Octavian in the eyes of the East. Additionally, Antony officially declared his alliance with Octavian over, proclaiming that from then on the East was free and independent of Rome. It was the worst blunder of Cleopatra's life.

A tetradrachm coin depicting Cleopatra

Chapter 4: A Death for the Ages

Between 33 and 32 BC, relationships between Rome and Alexandria steadily broke down. In Egypt, Antony and Cleopatra accused Octavian of not being Caesar's true heir, pointing out that Caesarion was Caesar's actual son, not his nephew, and thus the worthier man to bear his name – a dangerous statement for Octavian, whose main source of public support, especially with the legions, was their love for his deceased adoptive father. Antony also unilaterally divorced Octavia, disowned his children by her, and threatened to stop the grain supply to Rome, while Octavian demanded Antony answer for waging war on Parthia and Judaea without the Senate's consent. Utilizing public relations yet again, Octavian made accusations of outright treason, while infuriating the Roman mob with tales of the excesses that the no-longer-Roman Antony indulged in within Cleopatra's palace.

In 32 BC, Octavian declared war against Cleopatra, rather than Antony, a calculated move intended to ensure the Romans did not feel he was continuing the legacy of the fratricidal civil war. Perhaps Octavian overestimated his support, for Cleopatra and Antony were delighted to discover that both consuls and a full third of the Senate had decamped from Rome and defected to their side wholesale. The royal couple met the defectors in Greece, and for a while felt so secure in their position they even considered an invasion of Italy itself.

Their victory was to prove short-lived, however. In 31 BC, Octavian's forces set sail for Greece, and the legions there immediately went over to his side, spurred by the veterans in their ranks who had once fought for his adoptive father Caesar. Both Cyrenaica and Greece fell to Octavian, essentially without a blow struck, and Cleopatra and Antony were forced to retreat back to Egypt, where they rallied the Eastern navies and prepared to contest Octavian's passage across the Mediterranean.

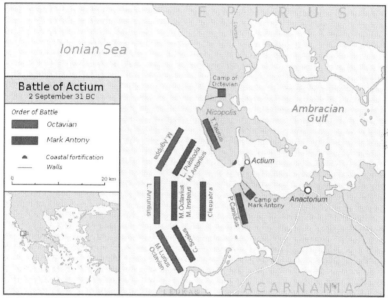

On September 2, 31 BC, Antony and Cleopatra found themselves in a tactically disadvantageous position, facing Octavian's navies off the coast of Actium, in Greece. With the risk of being bottled up and surrounded at Actium by Octavian's naval forces a very real possibility, Cleopatra advised Antony to give battle, although it appears the Roman general thought victory was an unlikely possibility. Antony and Cleopatra appeared, to the untrained eye, to have the advantage: their fleet numbered over 500 vessels, almost half of which were giant five-decked quinquiremes, ramming warships that carried full-blown siege engines on board, while Octavian had only 250 far lighter craft.

However, the sea was rough that morning, favoring Octavian's more maneuverable ships, which were less affected by the rolling swells, and to make matters worse, Antony's fleet had been wracked by disease, meaning that many of his mighty quinquiremes were undermanned. The giant craft were ponderous to begin with, but without the requisite number of rowers and fighting men, they could never hope to achieve proper ramming speed. Octavian's lighter, more agile craft, filled with veteran sailors, were able to dance around the ponderous quinquiremes, showering them with hails of fire arrows, ramming and boarding where they could, and sprinting away before the heavier craft had a chance to bring their rams to bear. As the day wore on, it became more and more apparent to Antony and Cleopatra, on their twin flagships, that the battle would be lost. More and more of their craft were being sunk, scattered or overwhelmed, and still more were burning down to the waterline, their skeleton crews being insufficient to man their battle stations and extinguish fires at the same time. As night approached, Antony and Cleopatra spotted a gap in the now thoroughly jumbled enemy line, and ordered their ships to speed through it without delay, making for Alexandria with all speed and abandoning their entire navy to its fate. It was a crushing blow, for Octavian and his generals had virtually annihilated Egypt's seaborne power.

17ᵗʰ century depiction of the Battle of Actium

As one of Rome's most famous battles, and one of the most famous events in Cleopatra's life, the Battle of Actium has taken on a life of its own in popular memory. One of the longest-held myths about the battle is that Cleopatra, sensing defeat, began to sail away from the fight in the middle of the day, and the lovestruck Antony followed her with his own ship, abandoning his men in the middle of the fight. While that popular myth would be in keeping with explaining Cleopatra's irresistible charm and magnetism, contemporary accounts of the battle do not suggest it was actually the case.

Actium was the decisive battle in the civil war between Antony and Octavian, but Antony and Cleopatra's troubles were far from over. They retreated to Alexandria, and Antony was still fairly certain he could give Octavian a run for his money on land – he was a famous, veteran commander, after all, and he had at his disposal 19 legions of infantry and more than 10,000 cavalry. However, due to a combination of disgust over his callous abandonment of his navy at Actium, a strong sense of loyalty to Caesar and his heir Octavian (and a healthy dose of common sense, in all likelihood), in August Antony's army deserted *en masse* and went over to Octavian virtually to the last man, leaving Antony and Cleopatra stranded in Alexandria, with just their personal bodyguard for defence, at the mercy of Octavian. Antony, furious at his army's betrayal, flew into a rage and raved against Cleopatra, declaring that she had betrayed him to Octavian in hopes of saving herself. Cleopatra was so terrified for her life that she locked herself away in her private rooms, and sent a message to Antony saying that, because she believed all hope was lost, she had taken her own life.

It remains unclear whether this was a callous act, deliberately engineered to drive Antony to commit suicide himself, or if Cleopatra was genuinely distraught and not thinking clearly. Whatever the case, Antony was so overwrought that he could see no other recourse than doing what any true, noble Roman would do in the event of his defeat - fall upon his sword. He made a botch of the job, however, giving himself a deep but non-fatal wound to the stomach. He laid himself down upon a couch, hoping that blood loss would carry him off, but as the blood flow slowed and the wound grew ever more painful, he began to beg for the release of death. Hearing of his plight, Cleopatra was horrified at what she had done, and commanded he be brought to her. Even in in his death throes, Antony was so happy to hear that she was alive that he consented, even though this required his being winched through a window, as Cleopatra had barricaded herself in her quarters. He died shortly thereafter, in her arms.

Cleopatra was so distraught over the note which had caused Antony to suffer such a painful and drawn-out death that she tore her clothes off, ripping at her hair and beating and scratching herself in her despair, before managing to achieve a measure of composure. She was captured by Octavian while praying over Antony's corpse, but though she was placed in the care of trusted men, Cleopatra would not suffer the final indignity of being paraded through the streets of Rome before the howling mob. As everyone now knows, Cleopatra famously took her own life.

Of course, the manner of Cleopatra's death has been debated for millennia, shaped in popular memory by everyone from Shakespeare to Hollywood. Ancient historians wrote that she had a venomous snake, most likely a cobra, concealed in her private apartments, and that when she realised that escape was impossible, she provoked it into administering a fatal bite on her arm. Today most people unfamiliar with those accounts believe that Cleopatra had an asp bite her on the breast, which was how Shakespeare depicted it in his famous play. Stories differ as to what snake was used (the term "asp" is most likely a generic name for any venomous snake, but Egypt is renowned for its deadly King Cobra) and if it was kept deliberately or came to be there by accident. Some historians even argue that there was no snake at all, and that Cleopatra poisoned herself with hemlock, as Socrates had done. Still others claim Octavian had her killed, which seems contrary to the widely-assumed belief that Octavian intended to parade her as a captive through the streets of Rome in a triumph.

The Death of Cleopatra by Reginald Arthur, 1892

Thus died Cleopatra VII, Thea Philopator, the last of the Ptolemies. Her line, which had lasted approximately three centuries, was extinguished with her. Her son Caesarion was almost certainly murdered soon after her death on the orders of Octavian, as all trace of him mysteriously disappears from the historical record, so the dynasty that Alexander's general had founded in the wars of the *Diadochii* came to an abrupt end.

Despite her own personal successes, Cleopatra's legacy was a ruinous one: her line extinguished, and her once independent (if subservient) kingdom reduced to a province governed directly from Rome. She had become mistress, in turn, to two of the most powerful men in the world, loved them in her own unique fashion, but betrayed one of them – Antony – in his gravest moment of peril. She was ruthless, strong-willed, arrogant in many respects, foolish in a great many others, and her political and military career, once she stepped out of the confines of Egypt, was a fiasco. Yet she was a remarkable woman for all that – anyone who has herself smuggled in a carpet past her rival's guards in order to snatch a crown from their fingers deserves admiration. Beautiful, reckless, cruel, and wanton – she was everything her enemies in Rome decried her as, but she was also ambitious, loyal, headstrong, and in many ways, wise beyond her years. Not the perfect woman, perhaps, but a great one.

Despite the tumultuous life she lived, Cleopatra remains a relevant and potent symbol as a strong-willed, independent woman who came to dominate two of the most powerful men of her age. And of course, much of the intrigue surrounding Cleopatra is a result of the mystique and uncertainty of her life and times, not to mention her very foreign religion and lifestyle. Though she died in the 1st century B.C., historians and archaeologists continue to search for her royal palace (presumed to have fallen under the sea after an earthquake) and even her burial chambers. Regardless, it can be safely assumed that people will still be talking about Cleopatra for many

years to come.
Bibliography

In addition to Caesar's commentaries, Readers interested in learning more about Caesar & Cleopatra should consult Plutarch's biographies of Caesar and Mark Antony, as well as Suetonius's *De Vita Caesarum*. Those interested in more modern reading should refer to Stacy Schiff's excellent *Cleopatra*, or Adrian Goldsworthy's *Antony and Cleopatra*.

Elizabeth I
Chapter 1: Early Life

The Lady Elizabeth in about 1546, by an unknown artist

Born September 7, 1533 at Greenwich Palace in England, as the daughter of England's sovereign King Henry VIII of England, Ireland and (nominally) France and his wife Anne Boleyn, Princess Elizabeth was born at a time of great strife in England. Her father Henry VIII had broken with the Holy Father, the Vicar of Christ, and the Catholic Church at The Vatican in order to annul his marriage to his first wife, Infanta Catherine of Aragon (later Queen Catherine) on grounds that part of the Book of Leviticus (stating "If a brother is to marry the wife of a brother they will remain childless.") forbade their marriage. This is because Catherine had been married to Henry's older brother and the erstwhile Prince of Wales, Arthur, but the Biblical passage had already technically been proven wrong by the birth of daughter Mary in 1516. Moreover, a much hoped-for Prince and male heir named Henry had been born in 1511, only to die after a few weeks as the infant Henry, Duke of Cornwall.

There were actually several reasons Henry sought to dissolve the marriage, using the religious one as a clearly faulty pretense. Henry believed that Catherine's inability to give Henry and England a surviving male heir made her a failure, and the ever-philandering Henry had become completely infatuated with Anne Boleyn. For those reasons, Henry clearly believed that he and Anne should marry in order to produce the next heir to the throne.

King Henry VIII

Unfortunately for Henry, Catherine of Aragon was a well-connected woman in Europe, which had made her such an attractive bride for Henry's older brother in the first place. The daughter of Ferdinand and Isabelle, Catherine was related to the Holy Roman Emperor, and the power players in Rome had no interest in dissolving Henry's marriage with her.

Catherine of Aragon

Henry had always been a believer in Catholic doctrine, so much so that he had taken great offense at Martin Luther's and later John Calvin's "heresies" and had published his own tract in defense of the Mother Church, a book fittingly named *In Defence of the Seven Sacraments*. But Henry put his own power and family's royal line ahead of his Catholic faith, and he took a number of steps to break with The Vatican. In a move that would have global repercussions for centuries, Henry founded the Church of England and became the new church's supreme head and governor, successfully exhorting Parliament to pass several acts so adjusting and thereby capitalizing on the English pride of self-determination (as opposed to the idea of foreign domination via The Vatican). Henry remained, in theological terms, "Defender of the Faith" (the title that the Church had conferred upon him and which the British monarch still retains). Elizabeth, who was not nearly as concerned about theological questions would still use Henry's brand of nationalism to unite her people during her monarchical tenure.

Anne Boleyn

By establishing the Church of England, Henry could make his own rules, so to speak, and he used the break with the Church to dissolve his marriage with Catherine. In 1533, Henry and Anne were married, but the honeymoon phase wouldn't last long, with tragic consequences for Henry's new wife. However alluring and seductive Henry had found Anne's playful manner *before* the wedding, he soon began to tire of her, due in no small part to her unbending, stubborn nature. Anne also had a nasty habit of political machinations, especially dealing with religion, which came at a time when religious divisions within England were at their peak. Most importantly, Henry believed Anne was a failure, just like Catherine, because she hadn't given Henry a surviving male heir. Elizabeth's birth had not been particularly welcome by Henry (who wanted a male heir for England to succeed him as the next ruler of the House of Tudor) or by Anne (who herself had deposed a queen consort and thus had set a dangerous precedent that could hoist her own petard).

Nonetheless, Elizabeth I's birth made her the Inheritrix Presumptive to the English throne at the time. King Henry VIII's elder daughter Mary (later to go down in history as "Bloody" Mary I of England, a staunch Catholic, and later a persecutor of Protestant "heretics") was delegitimized via Act of Succession 1533 (First Succession Act) upon Elizabeth's birth, and her life was made rather miserable. Mary was compelled to be a lady-in-waiting to the infant Elizabeth, the same infant who had replaced Mary in the line of succession. A greater humiliation would be harder to imagine. Elizabeth's place would not last long. Queen Anne's miscarriage of a male heir, upon hearing the news of her husband's hunting accident, made her especially vulnerable. King Henry VIII now had lost his patience with Anne, as he had with Queen Catherine.

Henry was caught in a bind, and his actions would affect his infant daughter's psychology for the rest of her life. Henry could not again afford a messy, long, drawn-out annulment process, and unlike Queen Catherine, who had had a powerful ally in Charles V, the Holy Roman Emperor, Anne's almost exclusively English ancestry conferred upon her no diplomatic or political leverage that might have given her protection against Henry's wrath. Henry had had Anne framed of various crimes, namely incest and adultery, under the alarming and death penalty-eligible headline of "high treason" against the King's Majesty.

Queen Anne was executed when Elizabeth was only two and a half years old. Throughout her life, her mother was a subject Elizabeth would be reluctant to discuss; it is likely the reason that Elizabeth would wait almost two decades before executing her subversive rival and cousin Mary, Queen of Scots, who was in Elizabeth's *own* custody. Naturally, and understandably, the perennial proximity of death to women who fell out of favor with the Establishment is a fear Elizabeth would carry with herself. Before Anne was executed, the Henry-Anne marriage was annulled by Henry himself as supreme governor of the Church of England. Elizabeth too was delegitimized.

After her mother's execution, Elizabeth saw her father marry four other wives, who were generally kind to Elizabeth. These wives — Jane Seymour, Anne of Cleves, Elizabeth's own cousin Catherine Howard, and the widow Catherine Parr — would make efforts to include Elizabeth and Mary in court, even though Elizabeth had been given her own household by her father. In her own young life, Elizabeth was blossoming: she learned to speak and write Greek, Latin, English, Scottish, Irish, Cornish, French, Spanish, Italian and Flemish, as well as learning how to conduct complex mathematical calculations. The Venetian ambassador to Elizabeth's court later would observe that Elizabeth "possessed [these] languages so thoroughly that each appeared to be her native tongue." Undoubtedly Elizabeth's emphasis on learning and cultural development had been informed by her own learning and value of erudition in manifold forms.

In the meantime, Elizabeth's young life was fraught with changes, often bloody and tragic ones. Queen Jane would die shortly after the birth of Elizabeth's half-brother and Henry's first surviving legitimate male issue, Prince Edward (later King Edward VI), in 1537. Edward incontrovertibly became the heir to the English throne, the third ruler of the Tudor dynasty. The humiliation that had been inflicted on Mary a la Elizabeth now was inflicted on Elizabeth a la Edward; Elizabeth was put in Edward's household and was commanded to carry the *chrisom* (baptismal cloth) at his christening. After Queen Jane, Henry would marry German grand ducal princess Anne of Cleves, a political marriage that Henry had regretted from the minute he laid eyes upon Anne. Henry quickly rejected her, but he did make amends by giving her Hever Castle (that had been Elizabeth's mother Anne Boleyn's family home) and a retinue of servants, as well as conferring upon her the title "The King's Sister." Elizabeth's next step-mother, Catherine Howard, would as a teenager be accused of "high treason" for consorting with her lover Thomas Culpeper. Henry had Anne Boleyn executed for fabricated incest charges, so naturally Catherine Howard lost her head for actual adultery. Henry's final wife and widow, Catherine Parr, skillfully managed Henry's choleric, irascible temper, and she got along well with Henry's children.

King Henry VIII died in 1547 basically a broken man and a magnificent ruler. His legacy of ruthlessness, ego and splendour was superseded in the public mind only by his founding of the Church of England and his six wives. To this day, schoolchildren know him by the latter (and by contemporary standards, unsavory) aspects of his legacy rather than by the intense complexity and confusion which attended Henry's split from The Vatican. Henry VIII was succeeded at first by Edward VI, but he had always been a sickly child much to his father's chagrin, and Edward would die in 1553 after just six years of reign.

King Edward VI

During Edward's reign, Elizabeth was the ward of her last step-mother, Catherine Parr, who subsequently married Thomas Seymour after Henry's death. Thomas was Edward's uncle and the brother of the Lord Protector, Edward Seymour. Seymour behaved inappropriately with Elizabeth, including entering her bedroom in his nightgown and slapping her on her private parts. Elizabeth found no protection even from her step-mother Catherine Parr, who turned a blind eye. Such conduct may well have turned Elizabeth off from the prospect of men, marriage and commitment, not necessarily because of what Seymour did to her but perhaps because Seymour's wife clearly had no control over her husband.

A strong Protestant, Edward did not want his crown to pass to Mary, a zealous Catholic whose brutal reign would include 280 "heretics" being burned at the stake during the "Marian Persecutions". However, Edward could see no constitutional, or indeed non-arbitrary way, to pass over Mary and instead choose Elizabeth. Hence, in his typical schoolboy penmanship, Edward's will attempted to override the Succession to the Crown Act 1543 (advocated by his father and passed by Parliament), barred *both* Mary and Elizabeth from the succession, and instead declared as his heir Lady Jane Grey, who was the granddaughter of Henry VIII's sister (and his father King Henry VII's daughter) Mary. Lady Jane was proclaimed queen by the Privy Council, possibly under duress, but her support soon waned after her own close blood relations distanced themselves from her, and she was deposed after just over a week.

Queen Mary I

Thus, the long-suffering Queen Catherine's legitimate issue with Henry, Queen Mary, rode victoriously into London — joined by Princess Elizabeth, perhaps for appearance's sake, perhaps for legitimacy's in order to send a message of sorts to her Protestant subjects — and was crowned. Mary's nod to Protestants turned out to be just lip-service, and she quickly began persecuting Protestants for their alleged heresies against the Holy Mother Church. Mary's Catholic faith, along with the scarring memories of how she and her mother had been treated by Henry VIII and the Protestant reformers, strengthened her resolve to destroy the Protestant reformation. It just so happened to be the same faith in which Elizabeth had been inculcated, a natural religious upbringing for the daughter of Anne Boleyn. Mary ordered everyone, including Elizabeth, to attend Catholic Mass (as had Henry); Elizabeth at least appeared to comply.

In 1554, Mary announced her decision to marry her staunchly Catholic cousin Prince Philip of Spain, the son of the same Emperor Charles V who had imprisoned the Pope and thus made impossible Henry VIII's annulment from Mary's mother Catherine. It was rather assumed that while it was purely political and dynastic for Philip, the marriage had those elements as well as infatuation, if not unequivocal love, for Mary. Philip, a Habsburg, married Mary and assumed the collective address: *Philip and Mary, by the Grace of God King and Queen of England, Spain, France, both the Sicilies, Jerusalem and Ireland, Defenders of the Faith, Archdukes of Austria, Dukes of Burgundy, Milan and Brabant, Counts of Habsburg, Flanders and Tyrol.*

Mary's English subjects were English first, and their religion was secondary to their collective identity. There was considerable distress and unhappiness among Mary's subjects over the marriage, partially because Philip was Catholic and partially because Philip was a foreigner. The formidable hydra of jingoism and nationalism reared its head. What now made Elizabeth's life increasingly difficult was that Protestant dissidents were making an icon out of her and presenting Elizabeth to the English people as a far superior alternative to Mary, who by this time had executed Thomas Cranmer, the influential Protestant Archbishop of Canterbury, and several others. About 800 Protestants read the tea leaves and went into self-imposed exile for their lives.

Mary I and her husband Philip attempted to retrench England back to the pre-Reformation era. Parliament repealed the Ecclesiastical Appointments Act 1534 and the Treasons Act 1534, which had made the monarch the supreme head of the Church of England, and basically disbanded the Church Henry had created. But because the powerful landowners who had benefited from King Henry VIII's dissolution of the monasteries were too influential, Mary and Philip had to accept that the lands and property would not revert back to the Catholic Church. Around January-February 1554, Protestant dissident Thomas Wyatt's rebellion broke out, and Mary's spies and government soon suppressed Wyatt. Wyatt had tried to enlist Elizabeth's help but either Elizabeth had refused or she had destroyed or successfully rebutted the evidence. Nonetheless, Elizabeth was summoned to court and was interrogated by Mary's senior officials regarding her part in the Wyatt rebellion. On 18 March, 1554, the Princess was imprisoned in the Tower of London.

By now, Elizabeth realized that her enemies wanted any excuse, even remotely credible, to frame her. The largely manufactured "high treason" charges with which Elizabeth's mother Queen Anne, her uncle Lord Rocheford, and her step-mother Catherine Howard were disposed of made clear to Elizabeth, especially in her formative years, that innocence counted for little against the monarch's accusation. Elizabeth powerfully maintained her innocence, and indeed it seems that it was somewhat-valid paranoia that had gripped Mary. The Holy Roman Emperor's ambassador Simon Renard advised Mary that her throne would remain unsafe so long as Elizabeth was alive; Mary's Chancellor, Stephen Gardiner, tried to try Elizabeth. In the government, Elizabeth did have loyal and powerful supporters, including Lord Paget, who persuaded Mary to spare Elizabeth's life since there was no actual, or even circumstantial, evidence against Elizabeth's conduct.

In late May 1554, Elizabeth was compelled to move gaols from the Tower of London to Woodstock, Oxford, where she was to be imprisoned for almost a year. During this time Mary underwent a fake pregnancy, which turned out to be a tumour and ended up taking her life. King Philip did little governing in England, but he realized early enough that Mary would be unable to give him and Spain a male heir and that Elizabeth would succeed Mary very soon. Therefore, Philip shrewdly helped spare Elizabeth's life during Mary's short regime.

Philip and the Habsburgs knew that Elizabeth's influence and power would become tremendously helpful and indispensable. However, this Philip-Elizabeth alliance would not last very long because Elizabeth would spurn Philip's marriage proposal. Instead, it would be the Catholic Philip, with the blessing of The Vatican, who would attempt to invade Elizabeth's England in 1588 by sending his Spanish Armada. But all that would come three decades later.

Philip II

On November 17, 1558, Mary I passed away, and Elizabeth succeeded her as sovereign. At her house in Hatfield, Elizabeth was greeted by senior ministers with the deceased Mary's signet ring symbolizing the marriage between the monarch and her kingdom (as Elizabeth herself would equate, "all my husbands, my good people"). Underneath a large oak tree, Elizabeth is noted to have said: "*Mirabile dictu*, this is God's will."

The rest of Elizabeth I's life had just begun.

Chapter 2: The First Part of Elizabeth's Reign

When Elizabeth ascended to the throne of England in 1558, many questions were looming, none more important than the Settlement Question about the Church of England vis-à-vis the Roman Catholic Church. Mary's rule had not been a particularly successful one and had torn England apart. The reign of Empress Matilda, the only other woman ruler centuries ago, was so distant and had been so short-lived that it had been long forgotten, so there was not much of a template for a woman ruler to follow, especially for a young 25 year old queen. As a result, Elizabeth would have to all but invent that role for herself, and she decided, probably early, that objective metrics of success rather than any definitive or stereotypical "female" imprint was the better path to follow, at least at that point in time.

Elizabeth also realized that her fidelity to her kingdom was important for yet another, though somewhat related and imminent, reason. She could unite the warring religious factions of English people under the obvious banner: England. This would have the effect of subordinating, perhaps even subsuming, the religious question under the more immediate identity of English-ness. Elizabeth made an example of her devotion to country, as she later would make an example of her famed virginity (becoming in lore a "Virgin" with a capital "v," thus replacing in the public *zeitgeist* the Catholic legend of The Virgin Mary), which inherently was brilliantly strategic. Elizabeth told Parliament in 1559: "And, in the end, this shall be for me sufficient, that a marble stone shall declare that a queen, having reigned such a time, lived and died a virgin." If Elizabeth, whether out of personal wishes or political expediency, could not bear a child and become a mother, a role beloved by her subjects, then she could reinvent herself as *their* national mother and defender. Thus she could and did gain their allegiance.

Elizabeth demonstrated her will and her inclusiveness in being everyone's mother, and she did so early in her tenure; her coronation was officiated by Owen Oglethorpe, the *Catholic* bishop of Carlisle, at Westminster Abbey, even after it was Protestants who had been instrumental in saving Elizabeth's life and her claim to the throne through the difficult years of Bloody Mary's reign. In government and religion, Elizabeth would steer a middle course, avoiding extremes — unlike her father and her siblings but very much like her late grandfather, Henry VII. Henry VII had realized, and Elizabeth, out of intuition or appreciation of the lessons of history, did too, that governing was a subtle art and possibly the subtlest of forms.

Elizabeth realized the virtues of filling the public vacuum on *her* own terms. This is a lesson Elizabeth would apply throughout her monarchical tenure. As far as devotion to England went, Elizabeth publicly demonstrated self-appreciation for the limits of her person's wishes. It was as if Elizabeth was making an importunate, though regal, plea that her quarrelling subjects follow her lead in putting England first, by separating her "body natural" from the "body politic":

> My lords, the law of nature moves me to sorrow for my sister;
> the burden that is fallen upon me makes me amazed, and yet,
> considering I am God's creature, ordained to obey His
> appointment, I will thereto yield, desiring from the bottom of my
> heart that I may have assistance of His grace to be the minister of
> His heavenly will in this office now committed to me. And as I
> am but one body naturally considered, though by His permission
> a body politic to govern, so shall I desire you all ... to be assistant
> to me, that I with my ruling and you with your service may make
> a good account to Almighty God and leave some comfort to our
> posterity on earth. I mean to direct all my actions by good advice
> and counsel.

Elizabeth was able to keep well-disguised her personal religious inclinations. Even though she herself was a Protestant, devout but not evangelical, Elizabeth kept Catholic liturgy largely intact. Notable Catholic symbols such as the crucifix were kept, and Elizabeth minimized the importance of sermons, a point of contention with staunch Protestant reformers. Yet Elizabeth, in a very real sense, *had* to be a Protestant because Catholic doctrine held that Elizabeth never had been a legitimate issue of King Henry VIII because, as some English Catholics believed and The Vatican certainly maintained, Henry's marriage to Anne Boleyn was null and void. Protestant doctrine was not enthusiastic about divorces and annulments, but it was more malleable from Elizabeth's point of view. Elizabeth had to balance the many religious and political factions on the religion question; her proposed compromise was to keep the monarch as the supreme governor of the church (the point that had meant the most to her father and had been anathema to

Mary) while allowing Catholic elements such as priestly vestments.

Elizabeth undoubtedly was helped by her good luck but it was also her strategy and artfulness and tact that had helped. Elizabeth was among the first English rulers to show that as important as *actions* can be, no less important are *inactions*. Silence on an issue and refusal to persecute or enforce shows at least as much about the design or priorities of the authority as does active enforcement or doing of some sort. Because of Elizabeth's clever manoeuvring and her immense good fortune, Parliament passed her proposed Act of Supremacy 1559, requiring all government officials to swear allegiance to the sovereign as the supreme governor or risk being removed from or ineligible for office; the heresy Acts so championed by Mary were repealed, in order to avoid persecution of dissidents that Mary had so fervently pursued.

Simultaneously, Elizabeth championed a new Act of Uniformity, rendering mandatory church attendance and the use of a new version of the Book of Common Prayer (1552). Under this new Act, the punishments for recusancy or the failure to attend church and comply with Elizabeth's religious laws were scaled down in severity.

Some of the advantages that Elizabeth's "virgin" status in the public imagination conferred upon her have been mentioned, but another advantage became evident only gradually over time. By postponing marriage until the point that it stopped becoming a chip she could credibly play, Elizabeth could hold foreign and domestic suitors at bay. This was an essential element in Elizabeth's foreign policy. The suitors had an incentive to cooperate with Elizabeth, sometimes with each other and always with England. Thus, Elizabeth entertained marriage negotiations, alongside her own personal love life (mainly with her childhood sweetheart Robert Dudley, Earl of Leicester as she herself later created him).

In 1559, upon finding herself on the throne, Elizabeth incurred her former brother-in-law Philip II's wrath by turning down his proposal of marriage. To stoke internal dissension among the Habsburgs, Elizabeth flirted with marriage negotiations between herself and Philip's cousin Archduke Charles of Austria. By 1569, however, Elizabeth's relations with the Habsburg dynasty had worsened. In order to stay in the game, Elizabeth considered marriage to two French princes of the House of Valois: first Henry (whom Elizabeth endearingly referred to as her "Frog Prince"), Duke of Anjou, and second, his brother Francis, Duke of Anjou, the erstwhile Duke of Alençon. The Francis, Duke of Anjou, proposal had to do with a possible alliance against Spanish control of the southern part of the Netherlands. None of this was surprising then since marriage alliances for monarchs concerned only dynastic considerations; love and attraction traditionally had a limited role to play.

In 1563 Elizabeth is reported to have told a foreign ambassador, "If I follow the inclination of my nature, it is this: beggar-woman and single, far rather than queen and married." If she did in fact say this, it is unclear if she said so in order to raise the market price of some Prince's getting her hand in marriage, or whether it was actually her genuine view on marriage. When Parliament exhorted her to marry in 1566 (upon her convening Parliament only because she needed Parliament to raise revenues by taxation), Elizabeth said, "I will never break the word of a prince spoken in public place, for my honour's sake. And therefore I say again, I will marry as soon as I can conveniently, if God take not him away with whom I mind to marry, or myself, or else some other great let happen."

Notice the flexibly-placed hedging word, "conveniently." The truth was that by 1559 it was abundantly clear to everyone at court that Robert Dudley was at the very epicenter of Elizabeth's romantic life. Even if she did marry, he would remain there. Elizabeth remained irritated with each of his wives, and when she died almost 20 years after Dudley's death, among her most private possessions was a letter from Dudley.

However, there was one obvious problem with having a "Virgin Queen". Throughout the early years of Elizabeth's reign, the succession issue came close to becoming the succession crisis. In 1563, after Elizabeth had almost died from smallpox but managed to survive due to what at the time was practically a miracle, her senior ministers as well as Parliament urged Elizabeth to marry or to select an heir that Parliament could then ratify. England was not yet free from the memories of the Wars of the Roses or the post-Henry VIII succession traumas. Still, Elizabeth was unwilling to follow either course of operation. Her logic was that just as her own very existence had been a threat to Mary, the nomination of a successor would similarly imperil Elizabeth's own life and throne. She would let history take its course, and eventually the son of Mary, Queen of Scots, King James I of England (James VI of Scotland) would succeed Elizabeth and unite the two competitive neighbors's crowns. The Tudor line that Henry VIII was so frantically desperate to keep alive with a male heir would die with his daughter.

Elizabeth may also have been warned by the reckless behavior of her rival for the English Crown, her own second cousin once removed, Mary, Queen of Scots, of the Stuart dynasty. Mary was the grand-daughter of Margaret Tudor, Henry VIII's sister. This made Mary a claimant to the English Crown as well. Moreover, her Catholicism made Mary the true and rightful Queen of England in the eyes of many Catholics and The Vatican. Mary's first marriage to the Dauphin of France had made her the queen consort of France, but his early death and their lack of issue had made it untenable for Mary Stuart to remain in France. Upon returning to Scotland, she married her cousin and gave birth to James VI. Mary Stuart, exhorted by her Catholic supporters, had claimed Elizabeth's crown.

Mary, Queen of Scots

This fact, coupled by the realization that several English Catholics, especially rebels active in the Rising of the North movement, supported Mary Stuart ardently made Elizabeth I uneasy. But Mary Stuart did not help herself when she married James Hepburn, 4th Earl of Bothwell, who had raped her. The Scottish people rebelled, and Mary abdicated and fled southwards towards England. Elizabeth I was unsure at first what to do with Mary, so Elizabeth kept her imprisoned in several castles and manor houses inside England (making escape difficult and thus unlikely). After 18 years and 9 months in Elizabeth's custody, it became clear that the situation was becoming untenable mainly due to Catholic efforts on the continent and within England to have Elizabeth I assassinated and to raise Mary Stuart to England's throne after marrying her to the recusant Catholic Thomas Howard, Duke of Norfolk.

After the Rising of the North rebellion was crushed, Elizabeth had 750 rebels executed. In 1570, Pope Pius V issued a papal bull (*Regnans in Excelsis*), excommunicating the "heretic" "Elizabeth, the pretended Queen of England and the servant of the Devil." The bull also emancipated all English subjects from loyalty and allegiance to Elizabeth. The bull went further: Catholics who complied with Elizabeth's orders would be excommunicated. However, the bull helped Elizabeth in that it pit England against foreign domination. Great leaders like Elizabeth know how to present a particular set of facts with a favourable spin. This was quintessentially so. Parliament, now incensed, passed laws against Catholics. This gave the mother-protector Elizabeth the chance to look magnanimous by mitigating these punishments.

In 1581, Parliament legislated to prevent the conversion of English subjects to Catholicism, directed with "the intent" to divert them away from being loyal to Elizabeth. Such an act was made a treasonable offense, carrying the ultimate punishment: the death penalty. Even though Elizabeth maintained in public that she did not wish to "make window into men's souls," terrorism (or what she and her ministers saw as terrorism) was a Kantian "categorical imperative" of an exception.

By some accounts, Elizabeth's spy master and principal secretary Francis Walsingham either trapped Mary or fabricated evidence on high treason charges associated with the plot initiated by Anthony Babington. In 1587, Mary was executed for her involvement in conspiracies to assassinate Elizabeth. Elizabeth is said to have had deep misgivings about executing a fellow sovereign and thereby setting a pernicious precedent. Nor had Elizabeth forgotten that her own mother, Queen Anne (though only a queen consort and not a queen regnant) had also been executed. Whether the rule of law protected rulers and others under the cover of sovereign immunity was now a dubious question. All this notwithstanding, Elizabeth also began to think that perhaps for a 16th female ruler there was wisdom in ruling and reigning alone, rather than alongside a husband.

Sir Francis Walsingham
Chapter 3: Final Part of Elizabeth's Reign

Unlike her father King Henry VIII, Elizabeth had no great ambition of increasing England's continental holdings. Most of her military were used for defense purposes. Part of the reason was that Elizabeth was not very concerned with expansion since preserving England's extant land was difficult enough. Another reason was that England's occupation of Le Havre, France from October 1562-June 1563 had concluded with an English defeat after England's French Protestant allies, the Huguenots, defected. The Huguenots had teamed up with the Catholics in order to re-conquer Le Havre.

Elizabeth had wished to exchange Le Havre for Calais, which she lost to the French in early 1558, but she did build on her father's idea of naval expansion. Through her fleets Elizabeth was able to pursue a more aggressive approach. When the war with Spain came, this strategy proved far more effective, when 80% of the fighting during that conflict took place at sea.

Characteristically, Elizabeth's strategy was subtle and multi-layered. She figured out that she could achieve England's goal of foreign riches while working toward the weakening or capitulation of other European powers if she let her pirates, as private commercial agents, raid foreign ships. By letting privateers do her dirty work, Elizabeth could then claim that her English government ships had been innocent of the deed, maintaining a form of plausible deniability that everyone could see through.

While she technically professed her innocence, Elizabeth did tip her hand in this regard when she knighted Sir Francis Drake upon his global circumnavigation. Drake became famous for his raids on Spain's ships, fleets and even ports (Spanish sovereignty notwithstanding). Elizabeth did play with fire here, and the piracy, along with the execution of Mary Stuart, gave Philip of Spain, as well as Catholic Christendom, a perfect excuse if not imperative to retaliate by attacking England. According to the Spanish and Holy Roman Empire's ambassadors, even if Elizabeth formally had little control over her seafarers, she did not have to encourage their transgressions.

Sir Francis Drake

Upon losing Le Havre completely by 1563 and until 1585 (a remarkable period lasting more than two decades), Elizabeth I eschewed expeditions on the European continent. In 1585, Elizabeth decided to send her army to help Dutch Protestants against her former brother-in-law Philip. Months earlier, in December 1584, Philip made a strategic alliance with the French Catholic League, which diminished the ability of King Henry III of France to block Spanish and Habsburg control of the Netherlands. The alliance also enhanced Spain's orbit of power over the channel coast of France.

This chain reaction meant that because the Catholic League was particularly potent along the French channel coast, England was now especially vulnerable to invasion. Elizabeth appreciated the strategic importance of what had happened and was incensed. In 1585, the Duke of Parma took Antwerp by siege and put the Dutch as well as Elizabeth on the spot, forcing her into action. Usually a greater believer in diplomacy over military conflicts, Elizabeth signed the Treaty of Nonsuch (1585), requiring her to contribute military support to the Netherlands when their self-defense needs so commanded. Now it was Philip's turn to be incensed. Elizabeth's efforts to keep peace eventually failed, for the Nonsuch Treaty subsequently gave birth to the Anglo-Spanish War. Only in 1604 (after Elizabeth's passing and James I's accession), with the Treaty of London, would this conflict cease to exist.

Robert Dudley, Earl of Leicester, led this expedition at Elizabeth's behest and in her name. From the very start Elizabeth did have her misgivings. Elizabeth did not mind playing a double game, so long as England and "all my husbands, my good people" were secure. Her delicate strategy, to promote the military interests of the Dutch at least up-front by lending them her troops, while simultaneously holding secret peace discussions with Spain, was completely at odds with Dudley's expectation that Elizabeth was committing all her energies to the Dutch cause. Dudley had been made aware by the Dutch of their expectation to actively fight the Spanish, but Elizabeth had other aims. More than anything, Elizabeth commanded Dudley "to avoid at all costs any decisive action with the enemy." With all these political and diplomatic machinations afoot, Dudley incurred Elizabeth's extraordinary and now-famous wrath when he took the post of Governor-General of the Dutch States-General.

Robert Dudley

The Queen saw through this and deemed this to be a Dutch tactic to compel England to protect the Netherlands by assuming de facto sovereignty over the Netherlands. Elizabeth did not want any more trouble on her hands, and she had studiously been avoiding this move. Being blindsided by Dudley's action, and now strategically and indirectly being forced to take this step offended her sensibilities greatly. Elizabeth made her annoyance lucid to Dudley, writing him, "We could never have imagined (had we not seen it fall out in experience) that a man raised up by ourself and extraordinarily favoured by us, above any other subject of this land, would have in so contemptible a sort broken our commandment in a cause that so greatly touches us in honour....And therefore our express pleasure and commandment is that, all delays and excuses laid apart, you do presently upon the duty of your allegiance obey and fulfill whatsoever the bearer hereof shall direct you to do in our name. Whereof fail you not, as you will answer the contrary at your utmost peril."

Amidst the explosive Netherlands situation came the real test of Elizabeth's reign, by which she would be remembered for centuries. Drake had attacked and humiliated Spanish ports and fleets, including those located in the Caribbean in 1585-86. In 1587, Drake had successfully attacked Cadiz, annihilating Spanish war ships intended by Philip to attack England someday. Now Philip and his Spanish court decided the hour of the Spanish Armada had come.

16th century depiction of the Spanish Armada

On July 12, 1588, the legendary Armada started for the English channel. The Spanish plan was to take this invasion, led by the Duke of Parma, to the coast of southeast England, where they would be released to conquer Elizabethan England for the Spanish monarch and Catholic

Christendom. The Armada included over 150 ships, 8,000 sailors and 18,000 soldiers, and it boasted a firepower of 1,500 brass guns and 1,000 iron guns. Just leaving port itself took the entire Armada two days.

As everyone who has been taught history now knows, the Armada was one of the most famous military debacles in history. Now whether it was simple mathematical miscalculation or plain bad luck, coupled with English fire ships assailing the Spanish Armada, the Aramada was defeated – decisively so. The Armada found its reluctant way home in awful conditions, having permanently lost over one third of the ships. On the Irish coast, the Armada had suffered further losses. Not yet knowing what had happened to the Armada, internal English gentry and militias sought to secure and protect England under Dudley's leadership. This is when Elizabeth I consolidated even further her image as mother-protector of her people. Inspecting her troops, long and to this day a regal tradition, at Tilbury on August 8, 1588, Elizabeth looked like a Greco-Roman war god. Adorned with a silver breastplate, she famously spoke:

> My loving people, we have been persuaded by some that are careful of our safety, to take heed how we commit ourself to armed multitudes for fear of treachery; but I assure you, I do not desire to live to distrust my faithful and loving people ... I know I have the body but of a weak and feeble woman, but I have the heart and stomach of a king, and of a King of England too, and think foul scorn that Parma or Spain, or any Prince of Europe should dare to invade the borders of my realm.

Elizabeth was hailed as a great savior of England, one who was willing to risk her own life to protect her children and her kingdom. In actuality, Elizabeth's luck had not been insignificant, but her preparations had also been immaculate, and indeed her pageantry had paid off. The monarch's procession to a service of thanksgiving at St Paul's Cathedral further solidified public support. Moreover, the vanquishing of the Armada became an unbelievably potent propaganda tool to warn away other sovereigns and kingdoms looking at England with desire.

This famous portrait of Elizabeth commemorates her victory over the Armada

The Armada's defeat was for Elizabeth and for England's Protestants a powerful triumph. Rightly or wrongly, the English people including many of Elizabeth's Catholic subjects who did not relish the idea of Spanish rule interpreted this victory as a manifestation of Divine favour and of England's sacrosanct status under its virgin ruler. In this, as intimated earlier, Elizabeth was playing on pre-Christian legends about the inherent sanctity and purity of virgins.

What was ignored in the middle of the celebrations was that the Anglo-Spanish War did continue and would continue until 1604. In reality, on the facts it seems that this conflict often did favour Spain. After all, the Spanish retained the Netherlands, thus hanging the scepter of possible invasion from that side. Another pirate, Sir Walter Raleigh, advanced the argument that, regardless of Elizabeth's grand and eloquent speech at Tillbury, it was her careful planning and subtle strategy that had stopped another full-scale war with Spain, stating, "If the late queen would have believed her men of war as she did her scribes, we had in her time beaten that great empire in pieces and made their kings of figs and oranges as in old times. But her Majesty did all by halves, and by petty invasions taught the Spaniard how to defend himself, and to see his own weakness." Elizabeth, it seemed, did not trust her generals all that greatly, Dudley being such an example. Elizabeth, for her part, claimed that once entrusted to fight on foreign shores her generals had a proclivity "to be transported with an haviour of vainglory." Of the Earl of Essex, Elizabeth wrote: "Where he is, or what he doth, or what he is to do, we are ignorant."

It is very interesting to observe Elizabeth's actions when Henry IV, a Protestant, came to the French throne in 1589. Of course Philip and the Catholic League challenged Henry's right to reign, and Elizabeth was indeed concerned about Spain acquiring the channel ports. Furthermore, England's later campaigns in France were messy and fruitless. Elizabeth's army of 4,000 men basically trekked around the northern part of France and produced nothing. This retinue, after halving down to 2,000 men, finally withdrew in December 1589. In 1591, another campaign (consisting of 3000 men) also was an English catastrophe. Elizabeth's fallacy lay in part in the fact that she refused to appropriate adequate funds for the supplies and reinforcements needed by the troops. An army of the Catholic League almost entirely destroyed an Elizabethan army in north-west France in 1591.

Given her opposition from the Spanish and Catholic League, Elizabeth tentatively approached France even though she was still seething from the Le Havre debacle in 1563. In July 1591, Elizabeth sent yet another army in order to aid Henry IV in laying siege to Rouen, but this too was a disaster. Henry IV gave up the siege in April 1592. In short, this French campaign too was an Elizabethan disaster, much like Le Havre twenty years ago.

Elizabeth was queen of Ireland, but its predominantly Catholic population naturally put up resistance, and Ireland always represented the threat of defecting over to the continental Catholics or to give them aid and comfort. Elizabeth's strategy was to allocate and grant vast estates to her cherished courtiers, thus stopping the rebels from lending Spain, Parma or other continental Catholics a military or economic base from which Elizabeth's England could be attacked. Whenever rebellions took place, Elizabethan armies swiftly were dispatched to engage in scorched-earth warfare. Sometimes they went to so far as to annihilate entire town populations by murder or starvation. One extreme case of the latter took place in the aftermath of a Munster revolt, when approximately 30,000 Irish people were killed by starvation. While the more appealing side of Elizabeth, possibly wisdom inherited from her grandfather, led her to require that the Irish be treated humanely, she seemed unfazed when the exact opposite happened. In Elizabeth's mind, this was an unavoidable cost of doing business in that era. By 1602, after several failed attempts, the Irish revolt was crushed, though Elizabeth did not live to see the final surrender of the rebel leader. Soon thereafter, Spain and England would become signatories to a relatively long-lasting peace treaty.

Elizabeth maintained friendly relations with Tsarist Russia, a relationship begun by her deceased half-brother Edward VI. Tsar Ivan IV wanted an ironclad military alliance, but Elizabeth would only go so far as engaging Russia in a commerce and navigation treaty. Elizabeth had done something similar with the Barbary States; she had "agreed to sell munitions supplies to Morocco, and she and Mulai Ahmad al-Mansur talked on and off about mounting a joint operation against the Spanish." Even in the most necessary of times, Elizabeth preferred not to enter into a standing military arrangement with any other power. Ad hoc military entanglements were the furthest she usually was willing to go. Ivan IV even sought asylum in

England, should his nobles and/or serfs rebel and fight him off the throne, and once proposed to Elizabeth I. Neither request was granted.

When Ivan IV was succeeded by his son Feodor, England's position in Russia became more precarious. Exclusive or almost-exclusive English trading rights in Russia were no longer acknowledged, and the English emissaries were ejected from the Russian court. Now at her wit's end, Elizabeth finally put forth the proposal of an Anglo-Russo military alliance, something she had up until now opposed, but Feodor rejected such an alliance. Even a great sovereign sometimes had to be flexible. As part of her deliberations with the Ottoman Empire, Elizabeth exported tin and lead and ammunitions to the Ottomans. Moreover, believing in the aphorism that an enemy's enemy is one's friend, Elizabeth actually pondered over the prospect of a collective military operation with the Ottoman Emperor Murad III when war with Spain came about in 1585. Catholics on the continent, notably Spain, were terribly alarmed. Murad and Elizabeth capitalized on this point by signing in 1580 a Treaty of Commerce and by conspicuously suggesting that Islam and Protestantism had "much more in common than either did with Roman Catholicism, as both rejected the worship of idols."

After defeating the Spanish Armada, Elizabeth still faced harsh problems. The Spanish and Irish militaristic engagements continued wreaking havoc, the tax imposition grew deeper and deeper, and inadequate harvests and war costs were taking a deleterious toll on England's economy. Prices and inflation increased, while standard of living decreased. For the first time in her reign, Elizabeth began to crack down on Catholic dissidents, probably because the external environment was so ripe for papal representatives and disloyal Catholic subjects to cause insurrections in the name of religion. In 1591, Elizabeth created secret commissions to target and interrogate Catholics.

To keep up appearances about prosperity and tranquillity, Elizabeth allowed spies and the propaganda machine to churn out convenient versions of reality. In her declining years, Elizabeth had lost much of her earlier cachet, and a casual corruption had seeped into her government. Much of the reason for this corruption was that Elizabeth, now nearing her 70th year, was unable to keep up with governmental intricacies, and she enabled her senior ministers to do much more of the governing than she once had. By the 1590s, a new generation of ministers ruled the Elizabethan court. Rival factions (particularly Earl of Essex and Robert Cecil, son of Lord Burghley), whom Elizabeth once had been quite competent to hold at bay, now contended with each other and jockeyed for control.

Portrait of Elizabeth circa 1600

In these final years, Elizabeth I could not summon the energies to wage external war as well as war with Parliament whenever she needed to raise revenue. Consequently, she began to grant, with greater frequency than ever before, monopolies instead of asking Parliament for subsidies. She saw this alternative as a costless way to gain patronage. The practical effects were artificial price-fixing, the enrichment of Elizabeth's senior ministers from public moneys, and of course public vilification of the system. Elizabeth, master politician to the last, spoke to Parliament in November 1601 on this issue. She pleaded ignorance of the details of the issue and made an emotive plea, "Who keeps their sovereign from the lapse of error, in which, by ignorance and not by intent they might have fallen, what thank they deserve, we know, though you may guess. And as nothing is more dear to us than he loving conservation of our subjects' hearts, what an undeserved doubt might we have incurred if the abusers of our liberality, the thrallers of our people, the wringers of the poor, had not been told us!" As usual, Elizabeth's pleas worked.

Not everything was doom and gloom, however. No matter how turbulent her reign may be viewed, given all the fighting with the Spanish and the manner in which she had even become Queen, what made (and continues to make) people so nostalgic for the Elizabethan Era is that this uncertain epoch also was the era of unrivaled cultural and literary development in English history. Indeed, around the beginning of Elizabeth's third decade as monarch, John Lyly's *Euphues* and Edmund Spenser's *The Shepheardes Calender* were published to much critical (and some public) acclaim. At the end of Elizabeth's reign (during the 1590s), Shakespeare and Marlowe had come into their own. In the theatre world, the Jacobean era during which the theatre arts in England reached their very apex and which followed the Elizabethan one was also the result of the latter.

Elizabeth patronized these art forms and artists, though not as greatly as some have assumed. Nonetheless this misimpression too was a result of Elizabeth's stature and the fundamental political truism that the authority in charge receives the credit and the blame (fairly or unfairly). In Spenser's poetry, Elizabeth became immortalized as the perennially young "Faerie Queene"; others called her "Gloriana." Despite the fact that Elizabeth had in fact become half-bald during her small-pox ailment in 1562 (the same one that gave rise to the fear of a succession crisis should the young queen die), she used make-up and glamour to her extreme advantage.

Chapter 4: Legacy

Queen Elizabeth I of England died on March 24, 1603 at Richmond Palace. Though she had put Mary, Queen of Scots to death, her unmarried and childless status left no Tudor to follow her. Thus, she was succeeded by her rival Mary Stuart's son James, whose reign united the two kingdoms of England and Scotland. All British monarchs have since descended from James.

Whether her reign remains such a fount of celebration -- even the Victorian age, not just the current Queen's reign, was compared with Elizabeth I's imperial majesty and success -- because of her immense good luck or her actual skill is perhaps a question never to be answered with complete satisfaction. What role poor leadership by subsequent kings played in making subjects nostalgic and interested in a revival of the Elizabethan Era is also unclear but certainly a factor. Nonetheless, Elizabeth I fits Shakespeare's description of Cleopatra (*Antony and Cleopatra*, II.ii.225–245): "Age cannot wither her, nor custom stale / Her infinite variety: other women cloy / The appetites they feed, but she makes hungry / Where most she satisfies."

One chronicler described Elizabeth I's Westminster Abbey funeral in these terms:
> Westminster was surcharged with multitudes of all sorts of people in their streets, houses, windows, leads and gutters, that came out to see the obsequy, and when they beheld her statue lying upon the coffin, there was such a general

sighing, groaning and weeping as the like hath not been seen or known in the memory of man.

Regardless of what credit she ultimately deserved, Elizabeth was remembered by contemporaries as an amazing figure, and she continues to be well regarded today. In the midst of the fighting with Spain, Pope Sixtus V remarked, "She is only a woman, only mistress of half an island, and yet she makes herself feared by Spain, by France, by the Empire, by all." As Elizabeth herself noted, "The love of my people hath appeared firm, and the devices of my enemies frustrate."

Mastering the game in a man's world, Elizabeth had positioned England to become Great Britain. Henry VIII had desperately sought royal stability with an heir, and it would undoubtedly have shocked him to watch Elizabeth provide it through a 44 year reign that united her subjects. The mother-protector had paved the way for Great Britain to become a global superpower that would dominate geopolitics for centuries.

Catherine the Great

Monument to Catherine in St. Petersburg

Chapter 1: Catherine's Childhood

Young Catherine soon after her arrival in Russia, by Louis Caravaque

"I will live to make myself not feared." – Catherine the Great

The woman who would become Russia's most famous queen was not even Russian. Catherine the Great was born Sophia Augusta Fredericka on May 2, 1729 to Prince Christian August of Anhalt-Zerbst, an officer in the German army, and Johanna Elizabeth of Holstein-Gottorp, daughter of the wealthy Duke and Duchess of Brunswick. Still a bride of 17 when her first child was born, Johanna was not entirely happy with her much older husband, and the sour relations between the two were only exacerbated by the difficult birth of Sophia. It took nearly 5 months for Johanna to recover from a childbirth that nearly killed her, and that simply piled onto a life that she found relatively bored compared to her earlier years growing up at court in Brunswick. While the child's parents had their marital strife, little Sophia would spend most of her first year of life being cared for exclusively by her wet nurse.

Christian August

Unfortunately, Sophia's life did not improve any when her brother, Wilhelm Christian, was born a year and a half later. Unhealthy at birth and crippled for life, he soon became their mother's favorite, and even after he died at the young age of 12, the devastated Johanna continued to show little interest in Sophia or her two remaining siblings.

While Sophia's mother had little interest in her children, their governess, Elizabeth Cardel, took her duties as primary caregiver much more seriously. Called Babet, Cardel inspired a lifelong love for the French language in her young pupil, though any romantic notions the young girl formed from French literature were carefully balance by the long passages of Scripture her German tutor, a local pastor, had her memorize.

By the time she was 8 years old, Sophia's bright and curious personality had attracted her mother's attention, and Johanna began bringing the child with her as she traveled to visit wealthier relatives. Both mother and daughter already considered Sophia a potential marriageable asset, which in this era provided the prospect of improving both of their lives. Though she was not considered a pretty child at 13, Sophia was showing the promise of growing into an attractive woman, and her quick intellect, leadership skills, and warmth made her an appealing potential match.

Johanna

Johanna's own status improved during the early 1740s when Christian August received a promotion to field marshal in the Prussian army and succeeded as ruler of Anhalt-Zerbst. The family now lived in a small baroque palace and was more financially secure than they had been in the past. With that, the options for a suitable husband for her daughter increased.

Chapter 2: Catherine the Bride

"A great wind is blowing, and that gives you either imagination or a headache." – Catherine the Great

One of Sophia's best prospects for a royal marriage lay in Russia, as Johanna's family had numerous ties to the Russian throne, currently held by the Empress Elizabeth, who had seized power in 1741. Elizabeth's older sister had been married to Johanna's cousin, and she herself had been betrothed to Johanna's older brother. Johanna wrote to Elizabeth expressing her congratulations in 1741 and the two began to correspond regularly. Elizabeth sent Johanna a richly jeweled miniature portrait as a sign of her favor and Johanna sent a portrait of Sophia in return and later asked Elizabeth to stand as godmother for her youngest child. Catherine the Great would eventually become known for her political intrigue and cunning, but it was her mother who was angling for her to become empress of Russia at this time.

Following her rise to power, Elizabeth named Peter Ulrich of Holstein, the son of her dead sister, Grand Duke of Russia. Then the Crown Prince of Sweden, Peter was pale, sickly and both emotionally and physically undeveloped for his age. He had poor manners, was uninterested in learning and loved to eat. He enjoyed military drills and playing with his toy soldiers, but he was not well enough for actual military training. He could speak French, Swedish and German, but he had no real aptitude for any other subjects. Peter enjoyed playing the violin, but had not been properly taught and therefore played poorly. After his father's death, an army official, Otto Brummer, took charge of his care, and Brummer was cruel to the boy, punishing him harshly and frequently refusing him food. Peter responded to this ill treatment by becoming both fearful and cruel himself, torturing animals and treating servants unkindly.

Peter

After naming him her heir, Elizabeth brought Peter to St. Petersburg at once, accompanied by Brummer, and she forced him to renounce his claim to the Swedish throne in favor of Russia's crown. She also assigned him new tutors and dancing and music instructors, but the harm to the young boy had already been done. Peter had no interest in anything Russian and actively objected to the notion of becoming Tsar of Russia. Instead, he remained firmly under Brummer's thumb.

In the meanwhile, Elizabeth named Johanna's brother heir to the Swedish throne and also contacted her friend about arranging a marriage between the future czar and Sophia, hoping that a German bride would help him to mature and focus on his duties in Russia. In January 1744, Johanna received a letter from the imperial court requesting she and Sophia present themselves as soon as possible, and the letter also included travel instructions and a letter of credit to cover the cost of the journey. Soon after, a letter arrived from Frederick II of Prussia clarifying that he hoped for a marriage between Sophia and Peter, and naturally Johanna was thrilled at her daughter's prospects.

Empress Elizabeth

Sophia's father, Christian August, was not invited to join the family, presumably because everyone believed that he would object to the match for religious reasons. While Russian royalty had, for centuries, refused to marry outside the Russian Orthodox Church, this policy had changed under Peter the Great. Thus, Sophia's Protestant upbringing would not be any hindrance to her marriage to Peter, and the absence of Christian August indicates Elizabeth and Frederick II clearly felt that Johanna could make this decision independently and would overcome any of her husband's objections. Christian August, who had always been fond of his daughter, gave his reluctant approval but left the details of planning the trip to his wife. As Johanna prepared to leave, she spent most of her travel budget on new dresses and items for herself, providing Sophia with a trousseau smaller than that of a girl from the local village. Even worse Johanna refused to allow Sophia to tell her beloved governess of their plan. Instead, in less than ten days, the family said their goodbyes and Sophia left for Berlin and an audience with Frederick II of Prussia.

Sophia said goodbye to her father 50 miles from Berlin. Both cried at their parting, and Sophia's letters home to her father show her love and respect for the quiet and modest man. Johanna and Sophia traveled on without him, taking only a few attendants and traveling under assumed names. The journey was a difficult one because the wet winter prevented them from using the quick-moving sleighs, but Sophia considered the journey a great adventure and was excited about the potential for her new life in Russia.

For his part, Frederick II, needed an alliance with Russia to shore up his nearly continuous war with Austria and saw the young German princess as a key means of creating that alliance. When they reached Berlin, Johanna presented herself but would not introduce Sophia. The king finally ordered the girl be provided with one of his sister's gowns and brought before him. Sophia sat alone at the king's table, where he found her both intelligent and charming. This was the only time the two great monarchs would meet.

Frederick the Great

A month after they left their home in Anhalt-Zerbst, the small party reached the Russian city of Riga and began to travel under their own names. The snow was heavier here, and they replaced their heavy carriages with elegant imperial sleighs, arriving in St. Petersburg on February 3, 1744. While the Empress Elizabeth was not present, mother and daughter were warmly welcomed by the court and outfitted with new Russian wardrobes in preparation for their eventual meeting with the Empress.

They set out a few days later for Moscow, hoping to reach the the Kremlin in time for Grand Duke Peter's 16th birthday celebration. The imperial sleighs moved quickly and the roads were good, allowing them to make the journey in only four days and arrive to a warm welcome in Moscow. Elizabeth had high hopes for the young princess, and, as she was a bit of a romantic who had chosen her lovers herself, hoped for a happy marriage for the two young people. Peter soon became friends with Sophia, but that was the extent of their relationship; Sophia soon realized that Peter was very much a child, more interested in games and toys than marriage or rule. Nevertheless, she was a remarkably practical young woman and played the only role she could in Peter's life, but her own memoirs present him as an unwise young man more than willing to display his love of Prussia rather than his loyalty to Russia.

Sophia chronicled Peter in a variety of negative ways in her memoirs:

"The Grand Duke appeared to rejoice at the arrival of my mother and myself. I was in my fifteenth year. During the first ten days he paid me much attention. Even then and in that short time, I saw and understood that he did not care much for the nation that he was destined to rule, and that he clung to Lutheranism, did not like his entourage, and was very childish. I remained silent and listened, and this gained me his trust. I remember him telling me that among other things, what pleased him most about me was that I was his second cousin, and that because I was related to him, he could speak to me with an open heart. Then he told me that he was in love with one of the Empress's maids of honor, who had been dismissed from court because of the misfortune of her mother, one Madame Lopukhina, who had been exiled to Siberia, that he would have liked to marry her, but that he was resigned to marry me because his aunt desired it. I listened with a blush to these family confidences, thanking him for his ready trust, but deep in my heart I was astonished by his imprudence and lack of judgment in many matters...

They raised the Prince for the throne of Sweden in a court that was too large for the country in which it was located and that was divided into several factions, which hated each other and vied to control the Prince's mind, which each faction wanted to shape. As a result, these factions inspired in him the reciprocal hatred they felt against the individuals they opposed...

From the age of ten, Peter III was partial to drink...

The education of Peter III was undermined by a clash of unfortunate circumstances. I will relate what I have seen and heard, and that in itself will clarify many things. I saw Peter III for the first time when he was eleven years old, in Eutin at the home of his guardian, the Prince Bishop of Lübeck. Some months after the death of Duke Karl Friedrich, Peter III's father, the Prince Bishop had in 1739 assembled all of his family at his home in Eutin to have his ward brought there. My grandmother, mother of the Prince Bishop, and my mother, sister of this same Prince, had come there from Hamburg with me. I was ten years old at the time.... It was then that I heard it said among this assembled family that the young duke was inclined to drink, that his attendants found it difficult to prevent him from getting drunk at meals, that he was restive and hotheaded, did not like his attendants and especially Brümmer, and that otherwise he showed vivacity, but had a delicate and sickly appearance. In truth, his face was pale in color and he seemed to be thin and of a delicate constitution. His attendants wanted to give this child the appearance of a mature man, and to this end they hampered and restrained him, which could only inculcate falseness in his conduct as well as his character..."

Sophia soon understood that she needed to please Empress Elizabeth more than Peter, and she set about immersing herself in the culture of her current country. She embraced her studies of Russia, both in terms of language and religion, and devoted herself to her study, even rising at night to practice the language. Her devotion to the language and faith impressed the court, and when she became ill the Empress herself nursed her back to health while Johanna ignored her daughter's needs.

On June 28, 1744, some months after she had recovered, Sophia officially converted to the Orthodox faith. At the ceremony, Sophia appeared pale and fatigued after three days of fasting, but she wore a scarlet gown made in the style of the Empress Elizabeth's and spoke well, reciting her vows in Russian. Her quick mind helped her to memorize the speech as she had so many others during her childhood. That day, Sophia became Ekaterina or Catherine, her new name chosen for her by Elizabeth. The betrothal ceremony, including costly rings presented by the Empress, took place the following day at the Kremlin.

Catherine soon had an income and a small court of her own but continued to function primarily as a playmate for her fiancé. When some courtier approached her and asked her to help correct his behavior, she refused, realizing that she needed to maintain his favor in the court for her own success. Meanwhile, Johanna was present in the court and at the betrothal but was displeased by the ceremony and her daughter's new rank as her superior in the court. As it turned out, Johanna had already been disgraced by her participation in court intrigues, and though Elizabeth continued to treat her well and send her gifts, Johanna was no longer welcomed at court. Her relationship with both her daughter and Peter also deteriorated during this time. In particular, Johanna disliked Peter and often took her rage out on her daughter, which actually had the perverse effect of bringing Peter and Catherine closer together once they began commiserating over the mistreatment they had both experienced. Unfortunately for them, Johanna would have to remain until after the wedding.

Peter's doctors, stating that the boy was not yet sexually mature, delayed the marriage by a full year, but Elizabeth still wanted to show off the future couple. In order to show her new family to the people, Elizabeth planned a pilgrimage across Russia, travelling by foot while the young couple held court in a carriage of their own. Johanna was horrified by the lack of court protocol, as was Peter's unwelcome supervisor, Brummer.

Portrait by George Christoph Grooth of the Grand Duchess Catherine circa 1745

While Elizabeth was fond of young Catherine, she was also a jealous woman. As Catherine's social status grew, Elizabeth became angry and lashed out at the girl over her debts. This was somewhat hypocritical since Elizabeth herself typically spent more lavishly than Catherine did.

In the fall of 1744, Peter contracted measles, and as soon as he recovered Elizabeth ordered the court moved from Moscow to St. Petersburg. Unfortunately, Peter was still weak and became ill once again, forcing Elizabeth to come to Peter and nurse the boy through smallpox for a six week period. Peter would not be well enough to reach St. Petersburg until late February of 1745.

Even as Elizabeth sat by Peter's sickbed, Johanna continued to cause problems in court. She objected to the fact that she and Catherine had separate rooms and believed Catherine's apartments were nicer than her own, which antagonized courtiers and also ensured Catherine and Johanna grew progressively further apart. Rumors began to circulate of an affair between Johanna and one of the counts in the court, and the events later that winter suggested the possibility when Johanna became pregnant and miscarried.

While Peter was sick and Johanna carried on, Johanna and Catherine were kept away from the boy out of fear of contagion, but when she finally saw her fiancé again, Catherine found his pock-marked face and body hideous. However, she had no intention of breaking her engagement; she was marrying the throne, not the boy who would inherit it. Even so, her reaction to his appearance destroyed their tenuous young friendship, and having been away from Catherine, Peter became even more child-like. Through much of 1745, Peter remained in his rooms, forcing his servants to engage in senseless military drills and playing with his toy soldiers. In May, Peter moved to the Summer Palace with Empress Elizabeth, leaving Catherine privately saddened by the lack of attention.

Against the wishes of Peter's physicians, Elizabeth set their wedding date for July 1745, despite the fact Peter's health continued to be frail and she needed a healthy, strong heir for the Russian throne. The wedding preparation began at once, with deliveries of cloth and other supplies as well as sketches and retellings of French weddings at Versailles. When the wedding finally took place on August 21, 1745, both bride and groom wore elaborate garments of cloth of silver. Catherine's memoirs described it as an exhausting and painful day, though she also noted that she still had her eye on the prize: "As this day approached, I grew more deeply melancholic. My heart did not foresee great happiness; ambition alone sustained me. At the bottom of my soul I had something, I know not what, that never for a single moment let me doubt that sooner or later I would succeed in becoming the sovereign Empress of Russia in my own right…"

Chapter 3: Catherine the Mother

"One cannot always know what children are thinking. Children are hard to understand, especially when careful training has accustomed them to obedience, and experience has made them cautious in their conversation with their teachers. Will you not draw from this the fine maxim that one should not scold children too much, but should make them trustful, so that they will not conceal their stupidities from us?" – Catherine the Great

Neither Catherine nor Peter was given any helpful or substantial instruction regarding marriage or marital intimacy. Peter had some vague, coarse conversations with his servants, while Catherine was unaware of even the most basic physical mechanics of sexuality. When Catherine asked her mother for information, she was harshly reprimanded, and when Peter finally came to bed on their wedding night, he fell asleep. The marriage would remain unconsummated for nine years.

There were most likely both psychological and physiological reasons for the couple's failure to consummate their marriage. Only two weeks after the wedding, Peter announced that he had fallen in love with one of Elizabeth's ladies-in-waiting. However, as the months passed and Catherine did not become pregnant, the blame fell on her shoulders. A woman, Madame Choglokova, was assigned to supervise the marriage bed and improve the marital relationship, but she made no attempt to do so. Catherine noted of Choglokova:

"At the end of May the Empress placed with me as chief governess Madame Choglokova, one of her maids of honor. This was a serious blow for me. I cried a great deal when she arrived and for the rest of the day; I had to be bled the following day. The morning before my bloodletting, the Empress came into my room, and seeing my red eyes, said to me that young women who did not love their husbands always cried, but that my mother had assured her that I had no aversion to marrying the Grand Duke, and that besides, she would not have forced me to do it, but that since I was married, I should not cry anymore.

The following day the Grand,Duke took me aside after dinner, and I saw clearly that he had been informed that Madame Cboglokova had been placed with me because I did not love him. But as I told him, I did not understand how they believed they would increase my tenderness for him by giving me this woman. Madame Choglokova was believed to be extremely virtuous because at that time she loved her husband adoringly; she had married him out of love. Such a fine example, placed before me, was perh aps meant to persuade me to do the same. We will see whether this succeeded.Madame Choglokova was a gambler. She urged me to play faro like all the others.

All of the Empress's favorites usually participated when they were not in Her Imperial Majesty's apartment. Besides this, also on behalf of Her Imperial Majesty, she gave me three thousand rubles to play faro. The ladies had noticed that I was short of money and had told the Empress. I asked her to thank Her Imperial Majesty for her Generosity."

Catherine reconciled with her mother after the wedding, but Johanna no longer served a role in the court and soon returned to Germany. The Empress sent gifts for her departure and gave Johanna a generous amount of money to pay her debts, and in return Johanna carried a letter to Frederick ordering him to recall his ambassador, indicating a clear break between Prussia and Russia. She left in disgrace and would, after the death of her husband, lose the small principality of Zerbst in Germany. Johanna died in exile in Paris.

Over the next few years, Elizabeth isolated the couple in the hopes it would force them to find solace in one another. While they did spend more time together, the nature of their relationship did not change, perhaps because they were closely supervised day and night. While Peter shared Catherine's bed, he played with his beloved toy soldiers, smuggled in by an ally in their small court. The situation within the court and their marriage did not improve and Peter grew progressively more difficult both personally and within their relationship, even maintaining a kennel of dogs in their room and routinely abusing the animals against Catherine's wishes and attempted interventions. Catherine wrote about one particularly strange anecdote that documented how difficult Peter could be:

"Toward the end of carnival, the Empress returned to the city. The first week of Lent, we began to make our devotions. Wednesday evening I was supposed to go bathe in Madame Choglokova's house, but the evening before, she came into my room, where the Grand Duke was too, and conveyed to him as well on the Empress's behalf the order to go bathe. Now, not only did he have a great dislike for bathing and all the other Russian customs or national habits, he even mortally detested them. He said quite firmly that he would do no such thing. She was also very stubborn and blunt in her speech, and told him that this would be disobeying Her Imperial Majesty. He declared that he could not be ordered to do what was repugnant to his nature, that he knew that the baths, to which he had never been, did not agree with him, that he did not want to die and that he held life most dear, and that the Empress would never force him to go. Madame Choglokova shot back that the Empress would know how to punish his disobedience. At this he became incensed. Finally she departed, saying that she was going to report this conversation word for word to the Empress. I do not know what she did, but she returned and the subject of argument changed, because she came to say that the Empress said that we did not have any children, that she was very angry, that she wanted to know which of us was at fault, and that she would send me a midwife and him a doctor. To all this she added many other outrageous remarks, of which we could make neither heads nor tails, and ended by saying that the Empress excused us from our devotions that week because the Grand Duke had said that the bath would undermine his health."

By 1750, Catherine and Peter returned to court in St. Petersburg, where Peter began a relationship with the Princess of Courland, a hunchbacked young woman. He also began to lash out at the Choglokovas and his aunt, and finally Elizabeth had had enough. The Empress announced she was sending a midwife and doctor to examine the couple, and now that the blame game was ready to start up, one of Catherine's ladies pointed out that since she was still a virgin, she could bear no fault, leading Madame Choglokova to in turn convince the Empress that the Grand Duchess was still a virgin. An experienced young woman was chosen to teach Peter about his duties in the marital bed, and though Peter was apparently successful with her, his interest in Catherine remained nonexistent.

Having endured several years of a loveless marriage, in 1752 Catherine became romantically involved with Sergei Saltykov, a handsome nobleman assigned to Peter's court. Peter became aware of the affair, but he was unconcerned by it and Madame Choglokova encouraged the relationship with Saltykov in the hopes Catherine might become pregnant. By December 1752, her plan had succeeded and Catherine was pregnant, but this pregnancy and a subsequent pregnancy both ended with miscarriages. Catherine documented her initial encounters with Saltykov in her memoirs:

"For some time already I had noticed that Chamberlain Sergei Saltykov was present more often than usual at court. He always came in the company of Lev Naryshkin. . . . Sergei Saltykov intimated to me the reason for his frequent appearances. At first I did not respond. When he spoke to me about it again, I asked him what he hoped to gain. He began to paint a picture as cheerful as it was passionate of the happiness he expected. I said, "And your wife, whom you married for love two years ago and with whom you are said to be madly in love, and she with you, what would she say?" He told me that all that glittered was not gold and that he was paying dearly for a moment of blindness. I did everything I could to make him change his mind. I truly believed that

I was succeeding. I pitied him. But to my misfortune I listened to him. He was remarkably handsome and surely no one equaled him in the grand court, much less in ours.

Meanwhile, Madame Choglokova, who always had her favorite project in mind, which was to ensure the succession, took me aside one day and said, "Listen, I must speak to you very seriously." I kept my eyes and ears open as one might expect. She began with a long disquisition, as was her wont, about her devotion to her husband, about her virtue, about what must and must not be done to love each other and to promote or support conjugal bonds, and then she pushed on, saying that there were sometimes situations of major consequence that should be exceptions to the rule. I let her say everything she wanted without interrupting, not knowing where she was going with this, a bit astonished, and not knowing if she was setting a trap far me or if she spoke sincerely. As I was having these private reflections, she said, "You are going to see how much I love my country and how sincere I am. I do not doubt that you fancy someone. You are free to choose between S.S. and L.N. If I am not mistaken, it is the latter." At this I cried out, "No no, not at all." Then she said, "Well then, if it is not him, it is the other no doubt." I did not say a word, and she continued, "You will see that I will not make difficulties for you." I played dumb."

Saltykov

By 1754, Catherine became pregnant again, but by this time Choglokov had died and his wife had been relieved of her duties. They were replaced by the Shuvalovs, relatives of Elizabeth's latest lover. After a slow journey to the palace in St. Petersburg, Catherine delivered a healthy son in the Empress' own apartments, and Elizabeth took the baby and the midwife at once, leaving the young mother in her labor bed. Hours later, Countess Shuvalov arrived to find that Catherine had not even been allowed a drink of water or moved into her own bed. The midwife finally returned, but Catherine was not allowed to see her son for a week. When Saltykov was sent on a diplomatic mission, Catherine found herself completely alone, and she wound up recovering from the childbirth in near total isolation, spending the winter in the small room in which she had given birth rather than her own apartments. Catherine recounted the isolation in her memoirs:

"After the baptism of my son, there were parties, balls, illuminations, and fireworks at court, while I was still in bed, ill and suffering great boredom. To cap it all, the seventeenth day of my confinement was chosen to inform me of two very unpleasant pieces of news. The first was that Sergei Saltykov had been named to deliver the news of my son's birth to Sweden. The second was that Princess Gagarina's marriage had been set for the following week. That is, in plain language, I was immediately going to be separated from the two people I loved most in my entourage. I sank more than ever into my bed, where I did nothing but grieve."

Eventually Catherine returned to court, and her public life changed considerably in February 1755. The birth of her son provided her with security and status as the mother of the heir to the throne, even if she was rarely allowed to see him, and though she remained helpful to Peter, she no longer went out of her way to please him. For his own part, Saltykov had gone to Sweden and enjoyed himself as the widely acknowledged father of the heir to the Russian throne. While they continued to correspond, their relationship was over.

Chapter 4: Catherine the Lover

"To tempt, and to be tempted, are things very nearly allied, and, in spite of the finest maxims of morality impressed upon the mind, whenever feeling has anything to do in the matter, no sooner is it excited than we have already gone vastly farther than we are aware of, and I have yet to learn how it is possible to prevent its being excited. Flight alone is, perhaps, the only remedy; but there are cases and circumstances in which flight becomes impossible, for how is it possible to fly, shun, or turn one's back in the midst of a court? The very attempt would give rise to remarks. Now, if you do not fly, there is nothing, it seems to me, so difficult as to escape from that which is essentially agreeable. All that can be said in opposition to it will appear but a prudery quite out of harmony with the natural instincts of the human heart; besides, no one holds his heart in his hand, tightening or relaxing his grasp of it at pleasure." – Catherine the Great

In June 1755, Catherine met a Polish count, Stanislaus Poniatowski, as well as an English ambassador, Sir Charles Hanbury-Williams. Hanbury-Williams would become a dear friend and trusted advisor, while Poniatowski, his secretary, would share her bed. Hanbury-Williams provided a much-needed paternal influence for Catherine, as well as financial assistance for the indebted princess, while Poniatowski was cultured, well-read, devoted, and fundamentally innocent. Saltykov had been a known womanizer, but Poniatowski was the opposite and thus a naturally appealing target for the young woman.

Poniatowski

During the winter of 1755, Peter continued to play with his toy soldiers, drink heavily and socialize with women of poor reputation. When he took an unwelcome liking to one of Catherine's ladies, she managed him by reminding him that if they argued, Elizabeth would dismiss his favorites. Her control of the wayward prince grew as she handled more and more of the questions and concerns regarding the administration of his German principality, Holstein, and in the process she personally grew more assertive and sure of herself. She even began to publicly question his lies and claims regarding his own prowess.

By 1756, Empress Elizabeth was ill and frequently debilitated to the point that her doctors feared for her health. Catherine, along with her allies, began to make plans for the succession. While Peter could not be removed entirely, she could take a role as co-ruler and handle the management of the country. Peter was already widely deemed unfit to rule and Vice-Chancellor Bestuzhev drew up documents for this arrangement, but Catherine refused to respond or acknowledge them in writing, instead thanking him verbally. While her refusal to support his plan protected her in the event it became public, she also objected to the key role he planned for himself in the administration.

Elizabeth made it known in 1757 that she had concerns about Catherine's involvement with Holstein. While she held no illusions regarding Peter's abilities, she continued to hope that he would improve his behavior. Removed from one of her key roles in the Grand Duke's administration, Catherine opted to throw Peter a grand party, defining herself a new role in the court.

On September 8, 1757, Empress Elizabeth suffered a stroke, and though she recovered quickly, her ill health became public news and the court could no longer hide her condition. In October 1757, the new French ambassador succeeded in removing Hanbury-Williams from his ambassadorial office, but Poniatowski remained in the country on his own merits.

Catherine delivered her second living child, a daughter fathered by Poniatowski, in December 1757. While she was again ignored in favor of the child, she had arranged her own labor and recovery rooms, as well as post-partum care. A large screen shielded a comfortable seating area so her friends could visit during her recovery and join her for meals during her confinement. While Elizabeth took the child at once, Catherine was less bothered than she had been with the loss of her son. When her daughter Anna died 15 months later, only Elizabeth and Catherine attended the funeral.

Equestrian Portrait of Grand Duchess Catherine

Chapter 4: Catherine the Politician

Vice-Chancellor Bestuzhev, who had been both Catherine's enemy and ally during her years in

Russia, fell from power early in 1758. With the support of the French ambassador (the Marquis l'Hopital), the head of the Secret Chancellory (Alexander Shuvalov), and Elizabeth's lover (Ivan Shuvalov), the Empress ordered Bestuzhev arrested. Several others in his close circle were arrested, and news of the arrests reached Catherine from Poniatowski. Bestuzhev's accusers had nothing specific with which to charge him, so they ultimately settled on a charge of lese-majeste or sowing discord between the Empress and the Grand Duke and Duchess. No evidence was found, and Bestuzhev was eventually allowed to retire to his own country estate.

Графъ Александръ Ивановичъ

ШУВАЛОВЪ.

Shuvalov

When Empress Elizabeth ordered Poniatowski recalled to Poland, he feigned illness and managed to remain in Russia, continuing to disguise himself and visit Catherine regularly. One night, as he returned from a nighttime visit, Peter's carriage met his and he was detained, but he was soon released with Shuvalov's assistance. However, his relationship with Catherine was now obvious to Peter, forcing Catherine to quickly intervene with Peter's mistress and cajole them into a warm and friendly conversation one night between the four of them. While Peter was pleased by this situation, Catherine realized that the very public nature of her relationship with Poniatowski placed her at additional risk and sent Poniatowski back to Poland herself, ending their romantic relationship.

Concerned with her personal loss and her own well-being, Catherine gathered all of her papers and burned them, asking her valet to witness the destruction. On the last day before Lent, Catherine announced she would attend the Russian theater, but Peter objected at once and refused her a carriage because he disliked the theater and wanted to enjoy the company of one of her ladies-in-waiting. In response to her situation, Catherine drafted a letter requesting permission to return home because her marriage had failed and asked Shuvalov to deliver it. Aware that the Empress could not send her home since she was a key political asset, this letter and what followed was a power play on Catherine's part, improving her access to resources within her own household and the court.

The following day, Catherine was informed that one of her few longtime attendants, Madame Vladislavova, had been dismissed. One of Catherine's ladies offered to try to intervene with her uncle and the Empress's confessor, Father Dubyansky, but Catherine feigned illness in order to meet with the confessor herself. While Catherine remained in bed, Father Dubyansky spoke with the Empress, encouraging her to meet with her one time protégé. Elizabeth granted her an audience on April 13, 1758.

Speaking in front of Ivan Shuvalov, Catherine again begged to be allowed to return home. Peter and Elizabeth were not receptive to her request, and Peter's behavior was so poor that Elizabeth called an end to the interview, privately telling Catherine that they would speak again. Alexander Shuvalov, who had heard the conversation while hiding behind a screen, visited Catherine's room some time later and assured her that she would have another audience with Elizabeth soon. When Catherine again met with Elizabeth more than a month later, the Empress treated her kindly and asked for details of Peter's life and behavior, but even though Catherine was restored to the Empress' favor, Peter still remained the heir.

As Elizabeth's health continued to decline, Catherine became a more prominent figure in the court, attracting the attention of Ivan Shuvalov. She also gained the support of Count Nikita Panin, her son Paul's tutor, and conspired with him to make Paul Elizabeth's heir rather than Peter. This would have made Catherine regent, allowing her to hold the throne herself through her son. Catherine also found an ally in Princess Catherine Dashkova, a popular court intellectual.

By far the most important of Catherine's new supporters was Lieutenant Gregory Orlov, a decorated soldier who soon became her secret lover. Orlov and Catherine were drawn together by physical passion, and in addition to the fact that their relationship was remarkably uncomplicated, with Orlov came the loyalty of his brothers and the guard they commanded. This immediately worked to Catherine's favor, as the Orlovs spread rumors about Peter among the ranks of the Russian Imperial Guard, saying that he was not only unfit to rule but loyal to his homeland of Germany and the empire of Prussia.

Orlov

In 1761, Catherine became pregnant with Orlov's child, and since Peter had been threatening to divorce her, she had no hopes that he would claim the child as his own. Thus she retired to her rooms and hid her pregnancy from the court. Meanwhile, Elizabeth was dying, and though she did not feel comfortable with Peter as her heir, she refused to change the order of succession. Catherine wrote, "It is impossible to say what Her Imperial Majesty Elizabeth Petrovna's last thoughts were about the succession, for she had no clear ideas on the subject. There is no doubt that she did not like P. III and considered him incapable of ruling; she knew he did not love the Russians, she thought of death with fear and horror, as well as of what would come after; but as she was slow in taking any decision, particularly in her last years, one can guess that she also hesitated on the question of the succession."

Prepared for the death of the Empress, Catherine even drafted a list of suggestions giving advice to Peter:

"1. It seems of the greatest importance that you should be informed, Sire, as exactly as possible, of the Empress's state of health, not relying upon hearsay, but with your ears wide open and with a complete grasp of the situation. If God disposes of her, you ought to be present at the event.

2. Having reached the scene and established that the event has taken place, you will emerge from her room, leaving behind you in the room a prominent national figure, who is capable of making all the arrangements suitable and customary on these

occasions.

3. With the self-control of a general in command of an army, without embarrassment or confusion, you will send for:

4. The Chancellor and other members of the Council, and while waiting for them:

5. You will summon the captain of the guards and make him take the oath of loyalty to you on the cross and the Bible (if the formula of the oath is not decided upon you will use that of the Greek Church).

6. You will order the captain (in case the General-Adjutant is not in a position to appear or you have found it opportune to leave him, as mentioned above in 2, with the Empress's body) to go and

7. Announce to the Court guards the news of the death and your accession to the throne of your forefathers according to the rights you hold from God and Nature, at the same time ordering."

In December 1761, the Empress suffered a massive stroke but remained lucid, taking the last rites of the Orthodox Church before dying on Christmas Day. Upon her death, the Grand Duke became Peter III, Emperor of Russia, and Peter wasted no time in throwing grand banquets and parties to celebrate his new role as Emperor, behaving childishly at the various funeral rituals and consistently refusing to follow Orthodox Church traditions regarding mourning and grief. Though by law he became the official head of the Church, he disliked any institution that sought to control his behavior and soon laid claim to much of its property, in addition to issuing orders deeply at odds with Church tradition.

Although his personal behavior was poor, Peter's political behavior was sometimes moderate and appropriate. He gave amnesty to a number of Elizabeth's enemies and reduced taxes. Always the wannabe soldier, he took an immediate interest in the military, ordering them into Prussian style uniforms and making peace with Frederick II of Prussia at once before preparing to attack Denmark. In the process, he had managed to make two powerful enemies in less than two months: the Russian Orthodox Church and the Russian army.

In April 1762, Catherine delivered a son who was immediately taken out of the city to be raised in the home of her valet, Vasily Shkurin, and within 10 days she had begun to take an active role at court once again. However, she and Peter remained on very poor terms, and he treated his mistress, Elizabeth Vorontsova, as Empress. He soon began to insult Catherine in public and even attempted to have her arrested on one occasion. After this, Catherine realized how tenuous her position was and began, to actively plot against Peter.

By June, Catherine and her co-conspirators had a plan in place. However, on June 27, only days before they planned to arrest Peter, rumors began to spread of the conspiracy. Concerned that they would be found out, Catherine's allies rushed to Peterhof to bring her back to the capital and proclaim her Empress, even before arresting and removing Peter from power. Early in the morning of June 28, Alexis Orlov, one of Gregory's brothers, woke Catherine and informed her of the situation. She left at once, with her hair undone and wearing a simple black dress, traveling in a shabby hired carriage pulled by farm horses purchased along the way to replace the exhausted team. Thus the future empress of Russia entered her capital simply and made her way immediately to the solder's barracks, where the regiment chaplain administered oaths of loyalty to all present while the Archbishop of Novgorod proclaimed her the sovereign ruler in St. Petersburg later that same morning. Paul, now Catherine's heir, arrived at the Winter Palace and he was formally proclaimed heir to the throne. Thus Catherine was made, not the regent, but the Empress of all Russia.

As for Peter, he had traveled to the country estate of Peterhof that morning and reached the deserted palace in the afternoon. When rumors reached Peterhof late that afternoon, he sent men into St. Petersburg, but when they arrived and faced the cheering crowds, they swore allegiance to Catherine. Later that night, Peter, believing that the fortress of Kronstadt was secure, moved there with his mistress and her ladies, only to find that he was not welcome and that the men at the fortress had, like so many others, proclaimed Catherine their Empress. Peter continued on, finally reaching the summer palace at Oranieumbaum, where he dismissed many of those with him, having learned that Catherine marched toward him with an army. In a last ditch effort to preserve his power, he wrote a letter to Catherine apologizing for his behavior and offering to share his throne.

Meanwhile, Catherine proclaimed herself colonel of the Preobrazhensky Guard and, dressed in a borrowed Russian military uniform, led the march herself toward Peterhof. As they traveled, a young member of the horse guard, Gregory Potemkin, broke rank to give the Empress the sword knot from his uniform to replace the one missing from hers, securing his own place in history.

Catherine in the Preobrazhensky Regiment's uniform

After camping overnight, the army again set off early the following morning, and along the way Peter's chancellor reached Catherine with his letter. When she stated that there would be no reply, he himself abandoned his Emperor and immediately took an oath of allegiance to Catherine. When Peter heard of this final defection, he formally abdicated the throne, asking only to be allowed to go to Holstein with his mistress.

Upon arriving in Peterhof, Catherine was informed that Peter was already there with his mistress, Elizabeth Vorontsova. After saying goodbye to his longtime companion, Peter asked to see Catherine, who refused the request and instead sent orders to imprison him. Peter was taken under heavy guard to a small country estate of his choosing, Ropsha, and Alexis Orlov was placed in charge of the prisoner until a more permanent solution could be found. While there is no evidence that Catherine ever suggested Peter be killed, those around her were more than willing to dispose of him, and within a week he was dead, strangled after dinner by his guards. Orlov sent news of Peter's death to Catherine in a hastily written letter that she kept locked away for the remainder of her life. For her own part, Catherine opted to claim that Peter had died of natural causes, perhaps hemorrhoids or the result of excess drink.

Chapter 5: Catherine the Empress

Portrait of Empress Catherine circa 1770 by Ivan Sablukov

"As a ruler, Catherine professed a great contempt for system, which she said she had been taught to despise by her master Voltaire. She declared that in politics a capable ruler must be guided by "circumstances, conjectures and conjunctions." - The Encyclopædia Britannica

Though Catherine's coup was widely supported and she had no significant opposition among the military or nobility, she did not have a legal right to the throne. Since the time of Peter the Great, the emperor could appoint a successor, but she had not been lawfully appointed by her husband. On top of that, her son Paul, still in the care of his loyal tutor, was often ill, causing more worry about her grip on power and potential succession.

Catherine also dealt swiftly with other matters in her court, both great and small. In order to shore up her power, she treated past adversaries leniently and showered her supporters with gifts, paying special attention to the Orlov brothers. While Gregory Orlov hoped to marry her, Catherine had no interest in marriage. Princess Dashkova was angered by her own rank in the court even after being promoted, and she frequently complained that she was seated among inferiors. Catherine recalled Bestuzhev and provided him with quarters in the summer palace, while her old enemies, including Elizabeth Vostokova, were treated kindly.

Catherine also planned a grand coronation for herself in the Kremlin in Moscow, and the ceremony that took place on September 13, 1762 lasted for more than four hours. She spent the next nine months of her reign in Moscow, where she made essential changes to maintain the key support she required to rule successfully. She canceled the Russian alliance with Prussia, recalled troops from Denmark, and ordered Russian soldiers home. She also returned church property secularized by Peter and restored the traditions of the Russian Orthodox Church, at least for a time.

While Catherine was able to maintain the support she required, the Russian government faced several key challenges. The treasury was bankrupt and the costs of grain had doubled, placing many of its people at risk of starvation. To alleviate some of this suffering, Catherine gave the funds allocated to her own household to the state treasury and banned all exports of grain to reduce the cost of bread. Within just a few months, the cost of grain dropped substantially, helping to ensure adequate food supplies, and her popularity naturally rose among the people. She also ended the monopolies on trade goods begun by Peter the Great to lower the cost of these items and increase competition. And Catherine regularly interacted with the Russian Senate, though it was known by all involved that she retained absolute power as monarch.

With Peter dead, there remained only one other possible claimant to the throne other than her own son and heir, Paul. Ivan VI was the infant king deposed by Elizabeth at the beginning of her reign. Raised in prison, he was mentally unstable as a result of his upbringing, and he was also uneducated, making him quite unfit to rule. However, Catherine's enemies could still proclaim him the rightful emperor, and when Catherine visited Ivan, she found him unintelligible, but not utterly disabled. Thus, she ordered his imprisonment to continue, placing Panin in charge of overseeing him, and Panin ordered no medical care be given to the young man in the hopes he would conveniently die of natural causes. And just to be safe, his guards, as they had been under Empress Elizabeth, were ordered to kill him rather than allow a potential escape.

In the winter of 1764, Vasily Mirovich was assigned to the isolated fortress that had been home to Ivan VI for many years. Mirovich was a bitter young man and saw Ivan as a potential means of gaining both fame and fortune. When Mirovich attempted to free the prisoner, the guards, as ordered, killed Ivan and brought Mirovich to trial, where he was condemned to death for his actions.

Mirovich Standing over the Corpse of Ivan VI (1884). by Ivan Tvorozhnikov

Though head of the Russian Orthodox Church, Catherine soon began to rethink returning the property Peter had taken. The Church was immensely wealthy, and Catherine was uncomfortable with that much wealth being in the hand of any institution she did not control. Claiming to want the Church to have more social responsibility to the people of Russia, she created a Senate committee to tabulate its total wealth. The Senate suggested that the Church retain its wealth but pay a higher tax to the state, and though the Archbishop of Novgorod offered his support for this plan, others in the Church did not. Their opposition was met in a way that would set the tone for much of her reign; Catherine silenced and imprisoned anyone who was too vocal with their criticism.

In 1764, she officially brought the Church under state control once again, placing more than one million additional peasants under state rather than Church care. Because taxing church property dramatically increased the wealth of the state, she had the strong support of the nobility, a largely secular population. With the loss of property and revenue, many churches and monasteries were forced to close, and priests and church officials were forced to rely on and become salaried employees of the state. The Russian Orthodox Church would never regain its former status and standing.

As early as 1766, Catherine began to revise the Russian legal code. The law code in place was already more than a century old and many new, often contradictory, laws had been added, creating both chaos and confusion. Peter the Great had made significant reforms, but he had not placed many of these into writing. Catherine's *Nakaz* or *Instruction of her Imperial Majesty Catherine the Second for the Commission Charged with Comparing a Project of a New Code of Laws,* took more than two years to develop. In the *Nakaz,* Catherine defined Russia as an absolute but moderate monarchy, with its power limited by tradition, including the dominant religion of the land.

Catherine called a National Assembly, drawn from all the free people of Russia, to create a new law code for the country. Delegates were paid a salary, depending upon their social class, and both the nobility and free working classes all had a voice in the Assembly. Of course, they were only there to offer advice, since Catherine retained the right to make any laws she chose but frequently attended meetings, secluded behind a curtain.

The *Nakaz* laid out reasonable punishments for crime, reduced the use of the death penalty and condemned torture. While her advisers objected, Catherine acknowledged the humanity and basic rights of the serf, even if she could not change their standing or status because of the objections of the nobility. In the original draft of the *Nakaz,* Catherine included measures to allow serfs to buy their freedom, limited servitude to only six years and required that once freed, a serf remain free. While Catherine embraced many Enlightenment ideas, the *Nakaz* was reviewed by the National Assembly and later, a number of nobles. All measures intended to improve the standing of the Russian serfdom were removed.

Nevertheless, Catherine's *Nakaz* was the first time the people of Russia, on however limited a basis, had been able to participate in the Russian government. It also demonstrated the influence that Enlightenment thinking was having on her, and Catherine ultimately became well-acquainted with Voltaire, who she respected and admired greatly. Excerpts from the *Nakaz* spell out just how important it was to Catherine that Russian rulers wield power as enlightened and benevolent despots:

"The Sovereign is absolute; for there is no other Authority but that which centers in his single Person, that can act with a Vigour proportionate to the Extent of such a vast Dominion.

The Extent of the Dominion requires an absolute Power to be vested in that Person who rules over it. It is expedient so to be, that the quick Dispatch of Affairs, sent from distant Parts, might make ample Amends for the Delay occasioned by the great Distance of the Places.

Every other Form of Government whatsoever would not only have been prejudicial to Russia, but would even have proved its entire Ruin.

It is better to be subject to the Laws under one Master, than to be subservient to many.

What is the true End of Monarchy? Not to deprive People of their natural Liberty; but to correct their Actions, in order to attain the supreme Good.

The Form of Government, therefore, which best attains this End, and at the same Time sets less Bounds than others to natural Liberty, is that which coincides with the Views and Purposes of rational Creatures, and answers the End, upon which we ought to fix a steadfast Eye in the Regulations of civil Polity.

The Intention and the End of Monarchy, is the Glory of the Citizens, of the State, and of the Sovereign.

But, from this Glory, a Sense of Liberty arises in a People governed by a Monarch; which may produce in these States as much Energy in transacting the most important Affairs, and may contribute as much to the Happiness of the Subjects, as even Liberty itself....

The Laws ought to be so framed, as to secure the Safety of every Citizen as much as possible.

The Equality of the Citizens consists in this; that they should all be subject to the same Laws.

This Equality requires Institutions so well adapted, as to prevent the Rich from oppressing those who are not so wealthy as themselves, and converting all the Charges and Employments intrusted to them as Magistrates only, to their own private Emolument....

In a State or Assemblage of People that live together in a Community, where there are Laws, Liberty can only consist in doing that which every One ought to do, and not to be constrained to do that which One ought not to do.

A Man ought to form in his own Mind an exact and clear Idea of what Liberty is. Liberty is the Right of doing whatsoever the Laws allow: And if any one Citizen could do what the Laws forbid, there would be no more Liberty; because others would have an equal Power of doing the same.

The political Liberty of a Citizen is the Peace of Mind arising from the Consciousness, that every Individual enjoys his peculiar Safety; and in order that the People might attain this Liberty, the Laws ought to be so framed, that no one Citizen should stand in Fear of another; but that all of them should stand in Fear of the same Laws....

The Usage of Torture is contrary to all the Dictates of Nature and Reason; even Mankind itself cries out against it, and demands loudly the total Abolition of it.

That Law, therefore, is highly beneficial to the Community where it is established, which ordains that every Man shall be judged by his Peers and Equals. For when the Fate of a Citizen is in Question, all Prejudices arising from the Difference of Rank or Fortune should be stifled; because they ought to have no Influence between the Judges and the Parties accused.

No Man ought to be looked upon as guilty, before he has received his judicial Sentence; nor can the Laws deprive him of their Protection, before it is proved that he has forfeited all Right to it. What Right therefore can Power give to any to inflict Punishment upon a Citizen at a Time, when it is yet dubious, whether he is Innocent or guilty?

A Society of Citizens, as well as every Thing else, requires a certain fixed Order:

There ought to be some to govern, and others to obey. And this is the Origin of every Kind of Subjection; which feels itself more or less alleviated, in Proportion to the Situation of the Subjects.And, consequently, as the Law of Nature commands Us to take as much Care, as lies in Our Power, of the Prosperity of all the People; we are obliged to alleviate the Situation of the Subjects, as much as sound Reason will permit. And therefore, to shun all Occasions of reducing People to a State of Slavery, except the utmost Necessity should inevitably oblige us to do it; in that Case, it ought not to be done for our own Benefit; but for the Interest of the State: Yet even that Case is extremely uncommon. Of whatever Kind Subjection may be, the civil Laws ought to guard, on the one Hand, against the Abuse of Slavery, and, on the other, against the Dangers which may arise from it.

It seems too, that the Method of exacting their Revenues, newly invented by the Lords, diminishes both the Inhabitants, and the Spirit of Agriculture in Russia. Almost all the Villages are heavily taxed. The Lords, who seldom or never reside in their Villages, lay an Impost on every Head of one, two, and even five Rubles, without the least Regard to the Means by which their Peasants may be able to raise this Money.

It is highly necessary that the Law should prescribe a Rule to the Lords, for a more judicious Method of raising their Revenues; and oblige them to levy such a Tax, as tends least to separate the Peasant from his House and Family; this would be the Means by which Agriculture would become more extensive, and Population be more increased in the Empire."

Still, Catherine was like any other 18th century monarchs in other respects, particularly when it came to expanding her empire. Poland, traditionally weak, was an easy acquisition, and since King Augustus III of Poland was dying without an heir. Catherine agreed to an alliance with Frederick II of Prussia to place her former lover, Stanislaus Poniatowski, on the Polish throne to succeed him. For some time after he left Russia, Catherine had remained emotionally tied to him, avoiding telling him of her involvement with Gregory Orlov or the birth of her third child. At the time Catherine became Empress, she still viewed Poniatowski as a powerful ally on the Polish throne. He was poor, would rely upon her for money and would remain loyal because he loved her. In short, he was little more than a political pawn. While she was not a fan of Frederick, these two great powers could together easily pressure the Polish nobility.

Catherine again intervened in Polish affairs two years later. Hoping to appease the Orthodox Church, she required increased religious tolerance in Poland. When Polish Catholics objected, causing significant unrest, she sent Russian troops into Poland, sparking a war with Turkey. While they were allies, as long as Catherine faced only a single enemy, Prussia was not required, by treaty, to respond. Frederick feared that the war might grow and sought a diplomatic solution, dividing more than a third of Poland between Prussia, Russia and Austria. The war with Turkey continued until 1774, when it ended with the Treaty of Kuchak Kainardzhi. By this time, Catherine had made substantial gains, particularly along the Black Sea. Turkey agreed to pay a substantial war indemnity and Catherine gained the right to trade freely in the seas under Turkish control.

Unfortunately, the peace was short lived. The second Turkish war began with a sudden declaration of war by the Turkish sultan in 1787, and Sweden also seized upon the opportunity, declaring war in 1788. However, Sweden lacked the forces necessary to succeed, and when the King of Sweden made astonishing demands, Catherine simply had to maintain the status quo in Finland. By the summer of 1790, the short-lived war with Sweden was over.

Meanwhile, Catherine still had to deal with Turkey. Austria was, by treaty, committed to the defense of Russia and Gregory Potemkin, now the head of the army, led the military response. The war continued with significant losses on both sides until the death of Joseph II, and after the war's conclusion, Austria signed an armistice with the Ottoman Empire. Peace between Russia and Turkey followed in the summer of 1791.

Chapter 6: Catherine the Mother of Russia

"Assuredly men of merit are never lacking at any time, for those are the men who manage affairs, and it is affairs that produce the men. I have never searched, and I have always found under my hand the men who have served me, and for the most part I have been well served." – Catherine the Great

The institution of serfdom began in late 16th century Russia to keep the serfs working the same plot of land, no matter who owned it. It also guaranteed them a number of rights and privileges that, over the next two centuries, were stripped away. Serfs could be bought and sold, families could be broken up without regard for their own well-being, and the serf lived or died as his or her owner chose.

By the time of Catherine's rule, approximately 1 million male serfs were under the control of the Church, half a million owned by the crown, 2.5 million by the state, and more than 5 million by the nobility. While most serfs were tied to land owned by the Church, state or nobility, others were the property of mines or foundries and had been since the time of Peter the Great. The lot of industrial serfs was significantly worse than that of those who farmed the land, as they worked in horrible conditions and their lives were short and harsh even by Russian standards. This state of affairs often led to riots.

Over a period of several years, Catherine, impacted by her own Enlightenment era studies on the natural rights of humans, considered the plight of these individuals. While she personally disapproved of the notion of serfdom, Catherine had little immediate recourse to end it. In 1767 she issued a decree regarding the nature of serfdom:

"The Governing Senate. . . has deemed it necessary to make known... that the landlords' serfs and peasants . . . owe their landlords proper submission and absolute obedience in all matters, according to the laws that have been enacted from time immemorial by the autocratic forefathers of Her Imperial Majesty and which have not been repealed, and which provide that all persons who dare to incite serfs and peasants to disobey their landlords shall be arrested and taken to the nearest government office, there to be punished forthwith as disturbers of the public tranquillity, according to the laws and without leniency. And should it so happen that even after the publication of the present decree of Her Imperial Majesty any serfs and peasants should cease to give the proper obedience to their landlords . . . and should make bold to submit unlawful petitions complaining of their landlords, and especially to petition Her Imperial Majesty personally, then both those who make the complaints and those who write up the petitions shall be punished by the knout and forthwith deported to Nerchinsk to penal servitude for life and shall be counted as part of the quota of recruits which their landlords must furnish to the army. And in order that people everywhere may know of the present decree, it shall be read in all the churches on Sundays and holy days for one month after it is received and therafter once every year during the great church festivals, lest anyone pretend ignorance."

As the tone of the decree suggests, serfs did not fare well under Catherine's reign, and she made no moves to improve the lives or conditions of either agricultural or industrial serfs. But she did tackle the question of their health and high infant mortality in part by establishing the first College of Medicine in Russia and recruiting doctors from throughout Europe to teach and work in Russia until native doctors could be trained. Each province was to have at least one hospital in its capital, and in Moscow there was also a specialized hospital dedicated to the treatment of sexually transmitted diseases. She also paid for a new lying-in and foundling hospital out of her personal income to reduce the rates of infanticide in Moscow. A system of baskets and bells allowed a mother to leave her newborn, without being seen, at a foundling hospital where conditions were good, with clean beds, ample food, and education. Children raised in the foundling hospital were guaranteed their freedom when grown and were given a vocational education to support themselves as urban citizens.

While Catherine herself rarely used the services of court doctors, the Russian state and Russian people still faced a serious threat. Smallpox killed without regard to social status or style of living, and in 1767 several members of the Austrian Hapsburg dynasty contracted smallpox, leading to multiple deaths. As a result, the Hapsburg empress Maria Theresa had her remaining children inoculated. At this time, inoculation required the injection of matter drawn from the pox of an individual with a mild, not overly serious, case of smallpox. It was still quite a new science and considered dangerous.

Fearing for the health of her son Paul, as well as her own well-being, Catherine invited Thomas Dimsdale, author of *The Present Method of Inoculating for the Small Pox*, to visit her court and explain his methods. She was vaccinated on October 12, 1768 and did not become seriously ill, merely developing a number of pox that healed within a week. She then had Paul inoculated, along with many of the Russian nobility. Inoculation clinics were soon established throughout Russia, and by 1780, more than 20,000 Russians had been inoculated against smallpox. Catherine's wisdom was confirmed when only a few years later smallpox took the life of the King of France, Louis XV.

While Catherine battled smallpox successfully, setting a valuable example for her people and promoting a life-saving inoculation, she could not fight another disease that would devastate

Russia during her reign. Bubonic plague, known as the Black Death in fourteenth-century Europe, struck Russia in 1770, and spread throughout the country over the next year. Catherine initiated quarantine procedures in an attempt to stop the spread of plague, but by fall the death toll in Moscow was as high as 800 people per day. The city was in chaos and the governor of Moscow wrote Catherine asking permission to leave. Gregory Orlov assembled a team and went to Moscow personally to manage the epidemic, resulting in a dramatic drop in deaths over the next few months.

While Catherine viewed herself as an Enlightened monarch, literate, cultured and thoughtful, the people of western Europe viewed her very differently. She was believed to be guilty of Peter's murder and implicated in the murder of Ivan VI as well. Moreover, Russia was widely considered unenlightened and certainly not fashionable. Catherine attempted to begin a correspondence with the French writer and philosopher Voltaire not long after she ascended to the throne, but Voltaire was reluctant to start a relationship, believing her rule would be short-lived. Eventually Catherine's communications got through, and the two eventually began a regular correspondence that continued for many years. Catherine wrote to the famous satirist, "Your wit makes others witty."

Furthermore, Catherine developed a relationship with the philosopher (and eventual encyclopedia author) Denis Diderot. While Diderot was well-known, he had not been financially successful, but late in his life Catherine purchased his entire library on the condition that it remain with him throughout his life. She also provided him a generous salary to care for it. When his salary was not paid on time by the Russian government, Catherine sent him fifty times the amount owed. Diderot, who quite disliked traveling, eventually made the long journey to Russia, where he and Catherine spent two hours together in lively conversation each day. As Voltaire hoped Frederick II of Prussia would become his ideal ruler of the Enlightenment era, so Diderot believed that Catherine could be his. But when he realized Catherine, while happy to have intellectual discussions, would not implement any of his many suggestions, he left Russia. Catherine hinted at the difference between philosophy and actual rule in one letter to him, writing, "You philosophers are lucky men. You write on paper and paper is patient. Unfortunate Empress that I am, I write on the susceptible skins of living beings."

Diderot

Diderot was the only one of the prominent French intellectuals of the Enlightenment that Catherine met, but she developed a lasting and significant relationship with Friedrich Melchior Grimm. Grimm, editor of the *Correspondence Litteraire*, journeyed to St. Petersburg with Paul's bride, Princess Wilhelmina of Hesse-Darmstadt and arrived in St. Petersburg shortly before Diderot in 1773. Like Catherine, he was German by birth, and the two became quite close, with Catherine even sharing her personal thoughts about the state, politics, and even her lovers.

By 1773, Catherine had weathered war, smallpox and the bubonic plague, and that year she would face an internal rebellion known as the *Pugachevshcina*. Led by the Don Cossack Emalyan Pugachev, disenfranchised people moved against the government, coming from far from the cities of Russia, along the steppes and in the Ural mountains. The Cossack populations in these regions had long resented imperial interference and had, because of their isolated nature, been largely self-governing. But during the Turkish war, they were more frequently recruited to serve in the army and were expected to pay taxes more regularly. Catherine first learned of the rebellion in October 1773, when Emalyan Pugachev claimed to be the now-dead former emperor Peter III. While Pugachev did not physically resemble the tall, slender Peter III, Peter had reigned for a very short time and his image had not circulated, making Pugachev's ploy at least one worth trying. Pugachev described an assassination attempt made by Catherine against him due to her objections to his plan to free the serfs. He promised that he would, as ruler, free the serfs, allow people to worship in the old ways, and provide salt and other commodities free of charge to all Cossacks. He even created his own court, naming friends after the nobles in St. Petersburg, and dictated imperial decrees to his secretary.

Early in the rebellion, Catherine paid it little attention and sent only a small force, since most of the army was occupied in Turkey. The region was typically unstable, so she initially figured this was just another manifestation of a minor, ongoing difficulty. But meanwhile, Pugachev and his army moved through the land, killing the nobility and villagers who remained loyal to the Empress. Towns began to surrender to avoid being plundered, and in January 1774 Catherine resorted to labeling Pugachev a "common highway robber".

By the spring of 1774, Catherine realized the seriousness of the situation and that she was faced with a full-blown rebellion. With much of the army still in Turkey, she created a loyal volunteer force that succeeded in breaking up Pugachev's army, but Pugachev escaped into the Ural mountains and remained in hiding for several months before reappearing with an army of 20,000 men in July of 1774, destroying much of the city of Kazan. The Russian army responded forcefully and successfully, forcing Pugachev to flee to the south as his men began to desert him. Forces under the command of Peter Panin followed Pugachev and his remaining troops, and by August the people along the Volga River were denouncing Pugachev as an imposter. He was defeated for the last time on August 24, but escaped by swimming across the Volga River. Panin finally captured him on September 30, 1774 and brought him before the empress that November. He was interrogated for six weeks, and eventually beheaded, drawn and quartered. Catherine issued a broad pardon thereafter, but many of her nobles responded violently against those who had rebelled. This impressed Catherine, and she kept in mind throughout the remainder of her reign that the nobles had supported her while the people had opposed her.

Chapter 7: Catherine the Matriarch

Catherine remained loyal and faithful to Gregory Orlov until 1772, when he shamed himself in the peace talks with the Turks. She decided to end the relationship and had a brief affair with a young man in the court, Alexander Vasilchikov, and when Orlov returned to St. Petersburg he found that Vasilchikov had taken his place. However, Vasilchikov, while attractive, soon bored Catherine, and in 1774 she began an affair with Gregory Potemkin. Potemkin was from a poor but noble family, and he was intelligent, thoughtful and well-spoken. After beginning his studies in the University of Moscow, he joined the army, and after his romantic gesture on the march to Peterhof, he was welcomed at court and frequently invited to social gatherings. He gained rank and served loyally for a number of years. Late in 1773, Catherine invited him to write to her privately, and the two engaged in a back-and-forth flirtation for some time before beginning a relationship in February 1774.

Potemkin

At once, the vainglorious Potemkin began to define his own rank in the court, aided by the fact that the two were passionately in love. Even today love notes between the two survive, often written and delivered from room to room in the palace. They spent several hours together each night, their apartments linked by a private stairway, and they may have married privately in 1774. Beginning in the late spring of 1774, Catherine privately addressed him as "my husband" and "my spouse". Their relationship continued for the rest of Potemkin's life, even after each would take other lovers.

Along with love came a sharing of power, and Potemkin took an active role in running the government from 1774 onward. In 1776, at Catherine's request, the Austrian emperor made Potemkin a prince of the Holy Roman Empire, and in the years that followed he gained control of much of southern Russia and improved conditions there. He took Catherine on a tour of these lands in 1787, revealing clean, newly built villages, vineyards and fields, but it was widely rumored that these were a pretense only meant to impress the Empress by hiding the unsavory state of things. In fact, the rumors took such strong hold that Potemkin is best remembered today for lending his name to the phrase "Potemkin Village", which describes something that superficially looks good in order to deceive viewers of the bare reality contained within. If it was a ruse, however, it fooled more than Catherine; contemporaries, including several ambassadors, shared similar descriptions of the positive conditions in southern Russia under Potemkin's supervision. On the same journey, Catherine met with Stanislaus Poniatowski, King of Poland, and Joseph II, Emperor of Austria.

While she still cared deeply for Potemkin, over the ensuing years their passion began to fade and Catherine started looking elsewhere. She began, with Potemkin's knowledge, a relationship with Peter Zavadovsky, who remained her favorite for only 18 months, and Catherine had a number of later lovers, but none served a political function. These men were chosen from her guard, enjoyed her favor and were quickly replaced. While the courts of Europe widely accepted affairs, Catherine's willingness to choose young men to entertain her was considered scandalous. Still, none took Potemkin's place, and when he became ill in the fall of 1791, Catherine was quite concerned. She was completely devastated when he died in October 1791.

Catherine had two living children but only acknowledged her son Paul as her heir, and she was careful to define him as her heir rather than Peter's to avoid any questions of paternity. Paul, who resembled Peter somewhat, was often ill, so it was decided that he should marry and hopefully father a child, just in case he died young. Catherine offered him the choice of three German princesses, sisters from Hesse-Darmstadt, and he chose Wilhelmina. As Elizabeth had done with Catherine so many years earlier, Catherine had Wilhelmina converted to Russian Orthodox and gave her the name Natalia. Paul and Natalia married on September 29, 1773.

Unfortunately, Natalia and Catherine had other similarities. Natalia was apparently unimpressed by Paul and spent too lavishly for Catherine's liking. Catherine often criticized her daughter in law until 1775, when Natalia became pregnant. The court prepared for the birth in 1776, but while the pregnancy went smoothly, her labor continued for five day before Natalia succumbed to the pain and blood loss. The male baby died with her. Catherine and Paul had remained with Natalia through the birth and were devastated by the loss, but Catherine eventually grew so tired of Paul's ongoing grief that she presented him with evidence of his wife's affair before her pregnancy. The Empress was much more bothered by the loss of a healthy male child and the burden of having to find a new bride for Paul.

With the support of Frederick of Prussia, Catherine chose Princess Sophia of Wittenburg as Paul's second wife. Now 17, the girl was already engaged, but that engagement was easily broken. Sophia was attractive, modest and good-natured. Paul traveled to Berlin to meet his future bride, and the fact that he was already enamored with all things German ensured that the trip improved the young widower's mood significantly. In September, Sophia, now called Maria, arrived in Russia, and she was quickly converted and betrothed. The two were married on September 26, 1776 and Maria delivered a healthy son, Alexander, only 14 months later. A second boy, Constantine, followed 18 months after, as did others, for a total of nine healthy children. Catherine took a significant role in the raising of Paul's first two sons, choosing their nurses, tutors and eventually wives. Paul and Maria were allowed to raise their five daughters and third son, born the year of Catherine's death.

Paul and Maria were happy together and it was a good match. In 1781, they toured Western Europe together, and when they visited Paris they were welcomed by Marie Antoinette and Louis XVI. But upon their return, Catherine criticized both of them, and Paul found that his beloved tutor, Panin, was dying. He soon learned that he would not be allowed to serve in the army or wield political power of any sort and became frustrated, often lashing out against those around him. Bereft of any important duties, Paul created a small private force of soldiers and put them through Prussian style drills, not unlike Peter III.

Paul was especially bothered by the role played by his mother's favorites and lovers in court. While he could have been crowned her co-ruler, Catherine viewed her son as competition rather than a potential asset. Over time, Paul became progressively more unbalanced until even his wife acknowledged that he was unwell. Catherine almost certainly considered naming Alexander her heir, bypassing Paul altogether, but if she produced a will to this effect it was ultimately destroyed rather than acknowledged.

In 1796, Catherine, at 67, was still lively and devoted to her work. On November 5, she rose as usual, but as she worked alone in her rooms she suffered a stroke. Paul and Maria, as well as others in the court, surrounded the dying Empress, and when the doctors told him she would not regain consciousness Paul ordered paperwork drawn up for his accession to the throne. Catherine the Great died on the night of November 6, 1796, and Paul had her buried together with the exhumed body of Peter III in the Cathedral of St. Peter and Paul, near the grave of Peter the Great. In her will, she requested, "Lay out my corpse dressed in white, with a golden crown on my head, and on it inscribe my Christian name. Mourning dress is to be worn for six months, and no longer: the shorter the better." Her wishes were fulfilled.

Chapter 8: Legacy

Catherine the Great had ruled for the better part of three decades, and she oversaw a considerable transformation of Russia during her reign, but Russia was still considered "other" by the Western Europeans, no matter how hard Catherine tried to cultivate the Enlightenment and claim it for herself and her people. For that reason, a general lack of information and the spread of rumors and scandalous information about Catherine led to an even more colorful and far more controversial legacy than the politically cunning, strong-willed Empress deserved.

Perhaps the most famous legends about Catherine surround how she died, the most persistent being that she died while attempting to have intercourse with a horse. The story is patently untrue, despite still being common today, and it was almost certainly inspired by the fact that

Catherine's contemporaries considered her sexual proclivities to be voracious based on the fact that she continued taking on new, young lovers well into her twilight years. In his epic poem *Don Juan*, Lord Byron's famous title character becomes one of Catherine's lovers when he's just 22 years old. In truth, when it came to her sexual activities, Catherine's behavior was so typical among monarchs of the period that it almost certainly received mention among her contemporaries only due to the fact she was a woman.

Another legend made reference to the fact she suffered a stroke in her bathroom, which got turned into her dying on the toilet (similar to the Elvis legend). Renowned Russian author Aleksandr Pushkin made a pun out of this story in an untitled poem, literally writing of Catherine in verse, "Decreed the orders, burned the fleets / And died boarding a vessel". But in Russian, the last line could also be translated as "And died sitting down on the toilet".

Indeed, the Western Europeans missed the forest for the trees, as Catherine was truly a remarkable and influential ruler. She modernized Russia from the inside, pulling in Enlightened ideals and overseeing the construction of new towns, her law code was progressive for the times, and her empire expanded in all directions, from Poland to Alaska. She admired Peter the Great, and in the end she emulated him, making it no surprise that Russians continue to look back fondly on Catherine and her reign as a Golden Age.

Bibliography

Massie, Robert. Catherine the Great: Portrait of a Woman. New York, NY: Random House, 2012

Rounding, Virginia. Catherine the Great: Love, Sex and Power. New York, NY: St. Martin's Griffin, 2008.

Queen Victoria

Chapter 1: Victoria's Early Years

Princess Victoria at 4 years old. Portrait by Stephen Poyntz Denning

On May 24, 1819, Alexandrina Victoria was born in Kensington Palace, London, to Edward Augustus, Duke of Kent [Edward Kent], and his wife Marie Luise Victoria, of Saxe-Coburg-Saalfeld, Princess of Leiningen, Duchess of Kent [Victoria Kent], a German aristocrat. This was Victoria Kent's second marriage; from her first marriage to Charles, Prince of Leiningen, in the German Empire she had already had two children named Carl Friedrich Wilhelm Emich, Prince of Leiningen and Princess Anna Feodora Auguste Charlotte Wilhelmine.

In order to understand Queen Victoria's life, it is important to understand the circumstances of her birth and upbringing. Princess Victoria was born into a family at war with itself and everyone else. They had been hemorrhaging power in the United Kingdom since the year 1714, when the German dynasty of the Hanoverians (the lower House of Wettin) succeeded to the British throne through King George I, a direct ancestor to Victoria. Her paternal grandfather King George III, known somewhat impertinently as the Mad King George III (which is still the subject of much historical fiction even in modern times) had gone insane, a possibility that would plague Victoria throughout her life. Especially during Queen Victoria's post-natal depressions, doctors as well as her family would suspect that the genetic disease had got hold of her. Little did they know that George III had had porphyria, whereas Victoria's condition was quite different indeed.

King George III

It might be said that Princess Alexandrina Victoria was even conceived to be Queen; at the time there was a palpable succession crisis in Britain. Victoria's first cousin and heiress presumptive, Princess Charlotte suddenly died in childbirth late in 1817. Charlotte's son was stillborn, and whether out of love for the late Princess or just out of a sense of national loss Britain went into mourning. George III's other sons, who were unmarried, raced to the altar to father an heir to the throne of Great Britain. Since the Prince of Wales, Prince Regent for the incapacitated George III, was separated from his lawful wife, the future Queen Caroline, there was no chance of a legal successor there. In order to incentivize the Georgian brothers to sire an heir, the bribe from Crown and Parliament was that their heavy debts – resultant from their Hanoverian excess – would be cancelled. Of course, from the days of George I the Hanoverian throne was bound up with the British one. The problem now was that Hanover, like most of the Continent at the time, had Salic law, meaning that women could not succeed to the Hanoverian throne. Thus, Victoria's uncle Ernest Augustus I, a son of George III, became King of Hanover, and the two thrones now diverged.

Even though another son of King George III, William IV, the Duke of Clarence (who would reign over Britain during 1830-37), did marry a minor German aristocrat, none of their children lived very long. After William was Edward Kent, who in rather a dastardly move (and yet preservative of ancestral ambitions) discarded his long-suffering mistress and married the German widowed duchess Victoria. Having had two children in her first marriage, she had given evidence of her fertility, so the risk of infertility was lower than it otherwise might have been. Of course, competition between the brothers and securing Parliamentary approval was high on the agenda, so the new Duchess of Kent needed to come to England. Debt problems made it difficult for Edward Kent to pay for the Duchess's safe passage, but eventually he managed to convey his court across the English Channel to Britain. At Kensington Palace, London (the palace that would eventually become the home of Princess Margaret and of Diana, Princess of Wales), Princess Alexandrina Victoria was born on 24 May 1819. The Prince Regent was unhappy with his brother Edward Kent and initially was unwilling to give him these grace-and-favour apartments. Princess Victoria was christened a month later.

This was an age of protocol where position, rank and etiquette mattered for their own sakes, authentic purposes notwithstanding. Since the Russian tsar Alexander I was young Victoria's godfather in absentia (a common phenomenon among the closely-related royal houses of Europe), the name "Alexandrina" was available. But the recalcitrant, though not necessarily contrary, young princess insisted on being called by her middle name of Victoria.

On January 23, 1820, Edward Kent died, leaving young Princess Victoria to be controlled and dominated by her mother the Duchess of Kent, who was emotionally and possibly romantically beholden to her Irish advisor Sir John Conroy. Conroy and the Duchess wished fervently for a Regency should King William IV, whose heir the young princess Victoria now was, happen to die before Victoria's 18th birthday. The King knew of the Conroy-Duchess aspirations, and he had no intention to submitting to the wishes of his ornery sister-in-law, the Duchess of Kent.

Conroy

Victoria would come to view her childhood years as "rather melancholy" due to the domineering ways of her mother and Conroy, who sought to use the heiress's prestige and young age to boost Conroy's personal fortunes. Even as a teenager, however, Victoria proved precocious, even as she was isolated from contacting those who were out of favour with her mother and Conroy. At the same time, the Duchess often made sure she and Victoria stayed away from the King's court because it was populated by his illegitimate children, which was a norm for the period but frowned upon by the Duchess. Even here, the subsequently Victorian theme of strict morality was evident.

Princess Victoria, 1833

Chapter 2: Albert

Despite the protective (or oppressive) nature of her mother, as the young princess grew older she naturally became more interested in suitors, of which there were obviously many. Victoria's uncle Leopold, King of the Belgians, sought to match his 17 year old niece to his other nephew (and Victoria's first cousin), Prince Albert of Saxe-Coburg and Gotha. Meanwhile, King William IV wanted the heiress to his throne to marry Prince Alexander of the Netherlands, the second son of the Prince of Orange.

Despite the machinations of the men, Victoria had her own opinions, which she shared with her diary. In it, the princess wrote that Albert "is extremely handsome; his hair is about the same colour as mine; his eyes are large and blue, and he has a beautiful nose and a very sweet mouth with fine teeth; but the charm of his countenance is his expression, which is most delightful." Conversely, Victoria characterized Alexander as "very plain". She later wrote to her uncle Leopold to thank him "for the prospect of great happiness you have contributed to give me, in the person of dear Albert ... He possesses every quality that could be desired to render me perfectly happy. He is so sensible, so kind, and so good, and so amiable too. He has besides the most pleasing and delightful exterior and appearance you can possibly see."

Albert, 1842

Marriage was not quite on the horizon in 1836, but a coronation was. On 20 June, 1837, the former Princess wrote in her diary, "I was awoke at 6 o'clock by Mamma, who told me the Archbishop of Canterbury and Lord Conyngham were here and wished to see me. I got out of bed and went into my sitting-room (only in my dressing gown) and alone, and saw them. Lord Conyngham then acquainted me that my poor Uncle, the King, was no more, and had expired at 12 minutes past 2 this morning, and consequently that I am Queen."

Upon succeeding to the throne of the United Kingdom, Victoria began to exert her newfound powers immediately. One of her first orders of business was to keep Conroy away from her, consigning him to the Duchess's house and keeping him out of the new queen's hair. In her early years, Victoria proved stubborn and willful, attributes not encouraged in a constitutional monarch and certainly not in a female constitutional monarch in the early 19th century. Moreover, it didn't take long for the young queen to make her mark by bringing down the government of Prime Minister Sir Robert Peel down in what is now known as the "Bedchamber

Crisis."

In 1839, Victoria's favorite Prime Minister, Viscount Melbourne, had resigned after Radicals and Tories voted against a Bill to suspend the constitution of Jamaica. This particular Bill took political power away from plantation owners who were resisting measures to abolish slavery in Jamaica. Peel had taken power; now the Queen was obstructing a traditional change at court. The Queen refused to give up her ladies of the bedchamber and gave what were perceived as petty slights to those whom she did not like. Many politicians and court advisors counselled Queen Victoria to marry, not for her own happiness necessarily but because a husband would rule over her unpredictable spirit and would help secure succession. A woman ruler at the time was not safe unless she could produce progeny.

As noted earlier, the royal houses of Europe were joined by blood and marriage. Victoria's mother and her brothers – one of whom, King Leopold I of Belgium, had been the husband of the ill-fated Princess Charlotte -- wished to keep the royal marriage with Princess Victoria within the family. Moreover, there just were not enough Protestant sovereigns, princes or grand dukes for Victoria to choose from. Victoria personally did interview many of them, which inherently was a revolutionary and ground-breaking move for a woman, even a ruler. Through it all, however, Victoria remained enamored with Albert. The Queen was bowled over by Albert's good looks and shy charm; indeed, she would retain this love for masculine beauty all through her life. She was also impressed by Albert's seriousness and meticulousness. For his part, Albert had endured a miserable childhood and family life, and it's possible he saw in the impressionable, intellectually inferior young British Queen a person to be molded to his better liking. Ironically, Victoria had Albert's education on her mind too, as she envisioned he would have to learn the proper protocols and ceremonial duties necessary of his position.

The Queen proposed – again, protocol dictated that no one could propose to her because of her rank – and they were married in February 1840. While it is true that there was enormous family pressure (especially from Leopold) for Victoria to marry Albert, she probably would have done so anyway. The Queen insisted that she would promise to "obey" Albert in her wedding vows. Even though she was the Queen Regnant, at home Victoria wanted Albert to be "master" and boss.

The marriage of Victoria and Albert, by George Hayter

However, this had its limits. It was at *home* and in *private* matters where Albert was boss, but all government and constitutional roles were Victoria's and hers alone. Victoria also had the keen political sense to realize that Albert's German roots would not play well among politicians, the British aristocracy or the people if Albert were allowed to meddle in politics, even slightly. At first, Albert only wielded the blotting paper as she signed official documents. Prince Consort Albert had always been persuaded to marry Victoria by his uncle Leopold, the carrot and prize being the great laboratory of England Albert would receive to execute his ideas through Victoria. He was therefore unhappy about his lack of job and status, for he too realized his intellectual potential and that this secretarial work was rather a waste of his talents.

Nevertheless, his primary function was to ensure the succession, which oddly enough offered him the chance to take a more hands-on role in things. When Victoria became so significantly pregnant that she could no longer maintain a ceremonial presence, Albert assumed her functions. There are those who argue that had Albert not died in his early 40's, he might have become something of a dictator. The Queen always had this importunate need to balance her maternal and wife role with her role of sovereign, a juggling act that sometimes got the better of her. After nine children in their first 16 years of marriage, Albert had established himself as her primary adviser, often drafting memoranda that she recopied in her own hand and signed.

Albert's abilities were so noteworthy and undeniable that even the curmudgeon Duke of

Wellington invited Albert to become chief of the army. This might have been Albert's great chance to affect public affairs, but he declined the offer, explaining that he had to subsume his ambitions in the interests of the Crown. Albert was successful in helping Victoria organize her work and efforts, to such an extent that Victoria would feel most helpless without him. From May 1 to October 15, 1851, Victoria would be immensely proud of Albert's Great Exhibition at the Crystal Palace in London. Its motive force was to foster significant change, with light streaming through its 293,655 panes of glass. *Six million visitors* came to see it, an extraordinary number at any time but especially in that era considering the geographical difficulties and the fact that was almost a third of the entire British population at the time. Charlotte Brontë wrote to her father, "Whatever human industry has created, you will find there."

Albert had the imagination to realize that the Hanoverian ancestors of Victoria had well-nigh sapped all the political power out of the monarchy, and that the real governors were now the Parliament. As a result, the validity and legitimacy of the Crown were dependent, exclusively, on the moral stature of the monarchy and the Crown's ability to encourage the arts and sciences. The Great Exhibition of the Works of Industry of all Nations was characterized as such: "Large, piled-up 'trophy' exhibits in the central avenue revealed the organizers' priorities; they generally put art or colonial raw materials in the most prestigious place. Technology and moving machinery were popular, especially working exhibits." Everything from the Indian Koh-i-Noor diamond to Samuel Colt's revolver to new daguerreotypes were on display there, and Victoria gave a speech that even moved Albert himself. Still, not everyone was pleased with the impressive (and excessive) displays.

During the Crimean War (1853-54), when the couple, especially Prince Albert, were suspected very falsely of Russian sympathies, this Victoria-Albert dual governance arrangement worked well. Because the royal houses of Europe were joined, England in any case was evolving, after the first Reform Bill (1832), into a constitutional monarchy, with the sovereign's powers becoming symbolic rather than legislative. The authority of the throne now rested more and more in popular respect for its occupant.

However, the arrangement ended abruptly when Albert, died in December 1861 of what was very likely stomach cancer. His physicians called it typhoid, but no other cases existed in the area, rendering that diagnosis suspect. Victoria was inconsolable by his death, and though Albert was aware that he had been suffering from an inoperable ailment, Victoria just could not understand it because her own constitution was so hearty and strong. His wife's mourning would last 13 years and would almost bring the monarchy down. Disparaging signs such as "To Let" would be hung from the railings and gates of Buckingham Palace at the absence of the Queen from public life.

Victoria's mourning and depression were not even a secret, and the queen referred to her feelings in a letter to American First Lady Mary Lincoln after the assassination of President Abraham Lincoln in April 1865. "No one can better appreciate than I can, who am myself utterly broken-hearted by the loss of my own beloved Husband, who was the Light of my Life,—my Stay—my All,—What your sufferings must be...." The widowed Lincoln would write back, "I have received the letter which Your Majesty has had the kindness to write., I am deeply grateful for this expression of tender sympathy, coming as they do, from a heart which from its own sorrow, can appreciate the intense grief I now endure."

Chapter 3: The Queen's Children

Before Albert died in 1861, the couple had given birth to nine children, and over the course of her long reign and her children's marriages, Victoria would earn the moniker "grandmother of Europe".

Albert, Victoria, and the children

Princess Victoria Adelaide Mary Louise (1840-1901) was the daughter whom the Queen probably *admired* the most. She married Friedrich Wilhelm of Prussia in 1858, who became the emperor of Germany but died after only three months of cancer of the larynx. He and Empress Victoria had shared a great, almost "English" instinct for liberalizing the stuffier Prussian imperial court in Germany. Indeed, this is why Victoria and Albert had arranged the match. Their eldest son became Wilhelm II of Germany (also known as Kaiser Bill of World War I), who became a most illiberal monarch and eventually led Germany to war *against* Britain in 1914. This contrast of intentions and reality — between Victoria and Albert's diplomatic ambitions and what actually transpired — caused tension and the dismantling of relations within the extended Royal Family, and it ultimately led to the renunciation of all German titles by Wilhelm's prickly British cousin King George V (Queen Elizabeth II's formidable paternal grandfather). Queen Victoria's favorite grandson was Wilhelm.

Queen and Princess Victoria, 1844

Princess Victoria had eight children in total. Her daughter Sophie went on to marry a Greek Prince and later became Queen of Greece. Princess Victoria passed away on August 5, 1901, of cancer, only eight months after the death of Queen Victoria.

Next came the child Victoria probably *despised* the most, a harsh but accurate assessment. **Prince Albert** (known as "Bertie" within the family) became King Edward VII in 1901 after Victoria's passing. From the beginning, Victoria and Albert imposed a strict regime upon their eldest son, but he had a rather creative and imaginative mind. Thus it should not have come as any surprise that he rebelled through over-indulgence in food, drink, women, gambling and sport. Victoria always blamed Bertie for the Prince Consort's death because the Prince Consort, upon hearing of young Bertie's sexual intercourse at the age of 19 with a young actress named Nellie Clifton in his military barracks, went to speak to him in Cambridge and got ill on his way there. To be fair, Albert probably died after a long struggle with stomach cancer and not his heartbreak over Bertie, but the Queen, in her irate and inconsolable state, was not interested in details. Nor was medical research advanced enough in those days. Bertie would always get the blame as far as his mother was concerned.

Edward VII in his coronation robes

At the age of 22, Bertie was married to the extremely beautiful but unintelligent Princess Alexandra of Denmark. Like most aristocratic and well-bred women in those days, Alexandra ignored Edward's extramarital affairs, of which there were no small number. Queen Victoria herself was shocked and alarmed that Edward was implicated in several divorce cases, the most infamous one of which concerned Lady Mordaunt. He had six children in total – Albert, George, Louise, Victoria, Maude and John. Maude went onto become the Queen Consort of Norway and George became monarch of the United Kingdom and oversaw British war efforts during World War I.

Princess Alice Maude Mary (1843-1878) was the Queen's third child. When she was 17, Queen Victoria decided it was time for Princess Alice to marry. She personally chose Prince Ludwig and Hesse as an ideal choice for her third daughter. Ludwig went on to become the Grand Duke Louis XIV, and within six months of arranging the introduction, they were married. Unfortunately, the marriage began in the shadow of Prince Albert's death (he had died shortly after arranging the introduction between Alice and Ludwig).

Alice went onto to have seven children – Victoria, Elizabeth, Ernst-Ludwig, Irene, Friedrich Wilheim (Frittie), Alix and Marie. Again, tragedy was to strike with the accidental death of her son Frittie. This loss weighed deeply on Alice and she went through a great depression. She mourned the loss until her own death and always talked about being reunited with Frittie in heaven. Her daughter Alix married Nicholas II, the last Russian tsar, and she would be assassinated along with her husband and children in 1917 by the Bolsheviks, thus ending the Russian royal house of Romanov.

Prince Alfred Ernest Albert (1844-1900) was Victoria and Albert's fourth child. Prince Alfred married the Grand Duchess Marie, daughter of Tsar Alexander II of Russia, and became the Duke of Saxe-Coburg. His eldest daughter Marie married the crown Prince of Romania, who later became King Ferdinand I.

Alfred was probably the most widely travelled of all his brothers and sisters. In fact, he was the first member of the Royal family to visit Australia. Unfortunately, during his trip in 1868, there was an attempt on his life in Sydney. An Irishman made the attempted assassination, and when it emerged that the would-be assassin was a Catholic, it only helped harden bigotry towards the Irish Catholics. Alfred's mother was to outlive him by a year – his death in 1900 was due to cancer of the throat.

The fifth child born to Victoria and Albert was **Princess Helena Augusta Victoria** (1846-1923). Princess Helena was also known as "Lenchen" in the family. She was born a "blue baby," possibly because her mother was at the height of anxiety over the loss of her first trusted Prime Minister, Sir Robert Peel. In 1866, she married Prince Frederick Christian of Schleswig-Holstein. The Queen insisted that Helena and Christian always remain with her and that Helena act as her private secretary. This was a condition before the Queen would consent to the marriage of Helena and Christian.

Princess Louise Caroline Alberta (1848-1939), the sixth child and one of only two of the Queen's offspring to see the hostilities of World War II against some of her own German cousins, was revolutionary in some ways. Although these days it is acceptable and does not really raise an eyebrow when British royals marry outside the community, as the Prince William-

Catherine Middleton wedding demonstrated, back then it was a conversation piece in gossip circles. In 1871, Princess Louise married John Douglas Sutherland Campbell, a commoner who would later become the Duke of Argyll.

Surprisingly, Princess Louise's engagement to John was supported not only by her mother but also by Benjamin Disraeli. Unexpectedly, the match also pleased the British public, which had feared yet another German marriage, which the general population felt had already occurred too often. Her husband became prominent in public life as an MP, and later on he became governor-general of Canada. The couple never had children, but they led an active and, by all accounts, pleasing and mutually satisfactory life together. This was undoubtedly one of the great-unsung royal love matches. When her husband died in 1914, Louise went into mourning and became something of a royal recluse until her own death in 1939 at the age of 91. Unlike Victoria's for the deceased Albert, Louise's grief for the departed Argyll was rather a settled resignation, which some might argue is a greater proof of love.

Prince Arthur William Patrick (1850-1942) was the seventh child born to Victoria and the Prince Consort. He married Princess Louise Margarete of Prussia. Arthur felt almost a sense of cosmic destiny that he was to join the armed forces, which he did, and he rose in rank until he was promoted in 1902 to the rank of Field Marshal.

One less-than-ideal fact about Prince Arthur was that he bore an unofficial allegiance to Germany, leading his brother King Edward to transfer him in 1911 to Canada, where he became the Governor General. His younger daughter, Princess Patricia, is well known to Canadians as Lady Patricia Ramsey, and Princess Patricia's Canadian Light Infantry is named after her. Prince Arthur became Grand Master of the Freemasons in 1901 when Edward, who had held that post, succeeded to the throne. He served as Grand Master until his death in 1942.

Prince Leopold George Duncan (1853-1884) was the eighth child born to Queen Victoria. Prince Leopold married the German royal, Princess Helena Frederica of Waldeck, but he was a hemophiliac and died two years after his marriage. He was known for his keen intellectual interests, his education at Oxford, and his befriending Lewis Carroll, John Ruskin and Oscar Wilde. His son became Duke of Saxe-Coburg, would later be declared a "traitor peer" for siding with Germany over the United Kingdom during World War II, and remains to this day rather a blot on the British Royal Family for being a core Nazi supporter of Adolf Hitler who ran the German Red Cross's extermination program for the mentally ill. Conversely, Prince Leopold's daughter Alice would go on to be a most beloved member of the British Royal Family into the 1980's.

Princess Beatrice Mary Victoria (1857-1944) was the youngest child of Victoria and the Prince Consort. The Princess was just four years old when her father passed away, and almost immediately Victoria turned to her youngest child as her only confidante, which must have been a source of inexplicable confusion to the young Princess. Queen Victoria's rather selfish objective was to keep Beatrice at her side at all times, and she destroyed a potential love match between Beatrice and the French royal Louise Napoleon when Beatrice was just a teenager. Beatrice would not have permission to marry for the next 11 years. Then she would be allowed to wed Prince Henry of Battenberg after much disagreement with the Queen.

The Queen again put on the table the condition that Beatrice and Battenberg live in Britain permanently. Battenberg agreed to the deal, and they married and had children. Beatrice was to pass on the hemophiliac gene to her sons and her daughter, Victoria, who would bring this gene into the royal family of Spain. When Battenberg contracted pneumonia and died, Princess Beatrice remained as a recluse on a cottage on the Isle of Wight estate of her parents. In 1944, amidst World War II, the Princess died after a long battle with rheumatism. Her children would rule Spain and her grandson Lord Louis Mountbatten would be the last Viceroy of India. Princess Beatrice's great-grandson, Prince Philip of Greece and Denmark, would marry Princess Elizabeth (now Elizabeth II), and sire the current Prince of Wales, Prince Charles.

Chapter 4: Changes in Victoria's Empire

As a teenager, Princess Victoria was taken by her mother on a royal progress through the country. Although the Duchess's intention was to avoid attending her hated brother-in-law King William IV's coronation, for the future Queen the trip was a joyous exposure.

Princess Victoria was stunned by the poverty and costs of the industrial revolution then raging in Britain: "The men, women, children, country and houses are all black...," she noted in her diary. "The grass is quite blasted and black." A blast furnace the entourage passed was "an extraordinary building flaming with fire," after which everything continued to be "black, engines flaming, coals, in abundance; everywhere, smoking and burning coal heaps, intermingled with wretched huts and carts and little ragged children."

The future Queen was also moved by the enthusiastic crowds, lengthy welcome addresses by local officials, choirs singing patriotic anthems, and salutes. In 1837, Victoria would comment astonishingly after seeing "the steam carriage pass with surprising quickness, striking sparks as it flew along the railroad, enveloped in clouds of smoke & making a loud noise. It was a curious thing indeed!"

Upon becoming Queen, Victoria allowed herself to be persuaded by Albert's philosophy that fascination with science and technology was desirable and that the Crown had to change with the world. At his request, the Great Western Railway constructed a state carriage for the Queen. On June 14, 1841, the Queen and Prince made their first journey in it (from Slough to London), thus setting a trend for their countrymen to follow. Queen Victoria was "quite charmed," but Albert was concerned that its speed of 50 miles per hour was too fast, even as Lord Melbourne dismissed these worries as absurd. Moreover, Victoria and Albert refused to take the royal barge often and preferred instead to take the new steamship *Trident* when returning from their favourite holiday home, Balmoral. All these changes became part and parcel of Albert's Great Exhibition in 1851.

Two wars had already emphasized to Britain the importance of long-distance telegraphic communication: the Crimean War in 1853-54, and the Indian Mutiny in 1856-57. No royal impetus was needed in those instances. But at Albert's death in 1861, his influence on the Queen, when it came to the engines of progress, ceased. Her attitude toward five later inventions which transformed Britain made that apparent, as she tolerated only three of them. In the later 1870s the typewriter began to revolutionize how people communicated on paper, but the Queen discouraged its use at her court. In January 1878 the Queen allowed Alexander Graham Bell to provide a demonstration of his newly-invented telephone, but her impression was not favorable: "It was faint." When commercial service began in London in 1879, she refused to allow a telephone in the living quarters in any of her residences. On top of that, electric lighting everywhere at Balmoral created more glare for her than visibility in her last years, as her fading eyes were afflicted by cataracts. She would have none of it in her private quarters at other residences. At her Diamond Jubilee in 1897 she found the electric light "very inefficient." The interested young woman inspired by her Prince Consort steadily give way to a dowdy, unchangeable older lady.

Chapter 5: The Business of Reigning

The Prince Consort's death altered the monarchy and the Queen irreparably. Victoria was inconsolable for a number of reasons. In addition to being shocked and at a loss, Victoria gradually came to realize that she had depended so long upon Albert's advice and support. With Albert gone, she became unsure she could reign alone.

In those initial years after his death, her long absence almost brought ruin upon her dynasty, and indeed the monarchy has never been *less* popular than it was in the 1870's. Not even during the 1997 shock and disgust over the monarchy's stiff-upper lip response to the death of Diana, Princess of Wales, was there a level of negativity comparable to the 1870s. Victoria's eldest son and heir Bertie, Prince of Wales, was intensely distrusted by his mother, so he was given no duties to cover for his mother's absence from public life. As noted earlier, Bertie's assignation with Nellie Clifton and Albert's shock over the affair, Victoria firmly believed, had caused Albert's death. In turn, this became a self-fulfilling prophecy, and Bertie became a womanizing playboy prince. Bertie almost died of typhoid fever, gaining him and the monarchy much public sympathy. Prime Minister Benjamin Disraeli, starting in 1874, flattered the Queen into opening Parliament for him and re-engaging herself in her duties.

Disraeli

The highly expensive Indian Mutiny in 1856-57 had led to reorganization of imperial rule in the subcontinent, and upon Victoria's return to visibility in the 1870s she desperately wanted to be acknowledged as "Empress of India." Disraeli and his Parliament were only too glad to oblige and subsequently conferred this title upon the Sovereign.

The Prince of Wales, eager for a trip to India, to hunt and hold court with the Nawabs, Maharajas, Maharanas and Maharaos, persuaded the Prime Minister to organize a tour. Bertie's easy charm made the trip a success, and he was an enormous success as an ambassador for the royal family and the monarchy and indeed the nation. On his way home, he found out that his mother, the Queen, had just been styled Empress of India.

Victoria had always been highly vulnerable to male beauty, but after Albert's death her sex life completely ceased to exist. To help her remember Albert, her advisors brought down from Balmoral to Windsor Albert's old Scottish gillie John Brown, a straight-talker who sat in on seances to channel the departed Prince Consort for the widowed queen. Brown got away with all as far as the Queen was concerned, and he is thought to have taught Victoria how to put a nip of Scotch in her tea. Ignoring class and other tools of stratification, Victoria awarded him a medal for loyal service, and when he died of natural causes, the Queen was heartbroken. "If he had been a more ambitious man," said Sir William Knollys, a member of the household staff, of John Brown, "there is no doubt . . . he might have meddled in more important matters. I presume the family will rejoice at his death, but I think very probably they are shortsighted." Brown's death brought Victoria sadness but it did make her public believe, again, that Victoria represented the middle-class values fitting for a national mother.

Chapter 6: Religion and Imperialism

The Victorian era is often given a negative connotation in the 21st century as being too stuffy, but in actuality Puritanism contradicted Victoria's lively character. After all, Victoria was queen in a transition that saw Britain's monarch become more of a figurehead than a ruler, and with that she worked to position the monarchy as a ceremonial caretaker who oversaw cultural customs and the like. Moreover, Victoria and her family had to live highly transparent lives in the equivalent of a fishbowl, making it all the more necessary to come across as personable.

In the same vein, the Victorian era is often considered an era of chaste morality, but Victoria, a true Hanoverian, enjoyed the sensual delights of matrimony, making it prudent for Albert to have a mechanical lock for their bedroom door at Osborne House installed within reach of his pillow. Albert and Victoria did not consider morality an absolute necessity because they were stodgy; they knew that the monarchy, in order to survive, had to set a moral example and be immune to even the potential for scandal. Victoria and Albert fell in love with middle-class Scotland and its Presbyterian values for this very reason, in contrast with English upper-class decadence and debauchery. A classic English aristocrat, Lord Melbourne declared to Victoria and Albert that this "damned morality would undo us all." In 1852, Albert observed, "We had found great advantage in it and were determined to adhere to it." She would write approvingly in 1855 of a sermon at a nearby kirk (Crathie Kirk) in which the sermon was: "Not slothful in business; fervent in spirit; serving the Lord."

Avoiding theological subtleties (which Anglicans were obsessed with), it focused on respectable conduct. Victoria's robust practical sense also admired the fact that this was not for "fourteen percent" Christians (church on Sundays, but no devout conduct the rest of the week), and it was "not a thing only for Sunday." Victoria held Albert's view that slavery should be banned, and in an overtly political move not readily imaginable by royals today Prince Albert, soon after getting married, became president of the Society for the Extinction of the Slave Trade and for the Civilization of Africa, in which he strikingly declared that slavery was "repugnant to spirit of Christianity." That the Christianity that arrived with the missions was a puzzling and culturally alien faith to Africans and Asians posed no problems to missionaries and the churches that supported them at home, but the Queen gave ambivalent signs as to what she thought of the presence of missionaries in Africa. At the same time, the British government, irrespective of the Prime Minister in office, wanted the missionaries to keep a low profile because deep passions were stirred by religious conversion processes.

When it came to religious faith, Victoria was always a believer in God and in some form of posthumous spiritual existence, hence the reason she conducted quite a few séances to reach her beloved Albert. In June 1850, when Lord Ashley, later the seventh Earl of Shaftesbury, was campaigning against the delivery of the Royal Mail on Sundays, she wrote to a Cabinet minister that she thought it was "a very false notion of obeying God's will, to do what will be the cause of much annoyance and possibly of great distress to private families." The Queen had fallen back on her practical religiosity. Along similar lines, Victoria vigorously abhorred the Evangelical campaign to ban public band concerts in the parks on Sundays, as she (who loved the arts) believed it was one of the few recreational chances for ordinary people.

The Queen exhibited only a few of the prejudices of her people. She was hostile toward the Papacy and Roman Catholics. She was not at all anti-Semitic, or at least far less so than most of her subjects and courtiers. The only evidence of anti-Semitism that some have come up with is the Queen's refusal to raise the banker Lionel de Rothschild to a peerage, but this was likely done only because the Queen considered his lending practices to be tantamount to legalized gambling. By the mid-1880's, Lionel's son Nathaniel was granted the peerage that Her Majesty had refused his father. The Queen had evolved, if she had ever been dated on the point at all.

Part of the stuffiness of the Victorian court was the Queen's refusal to allow anyone else to be effusive or sentimental, though she embodied both of these attributes all her life. In fact, after the Prince Consort's death this reached a crescendo. Victoria detested Prime Minister William Ewart Gladstone's overt piety, as well as his late-night rescue missions to save children and ladies of the night from their own miseries. Gladstone wore his religious and social conscience on his sleeve and walked the streets at night to confront desperate prostitutes, go with them to their rooms, and offer them Bibles and money to convert to a moral life. The Queen did not appreciate these gestures and required Gladstone to wear a fresh batch of clothes every time he came to see her!

Victoria was also socially conservative enough to consider divorce anathema. Victoria's perspective was so sheltered that she almost refused to approve the Criminal Law Amendment Act of 1885, which criminalized sex offenses against women and raised the age of consent. But it also criminalized acts of "gross indecency", which was a vague term but still offensive to Victoria's sensibilities, as she could not bring herself to believe that "women [could] do such things." The monarchy was important enough at the time in order for the Amendment to be changed to apply only to males, not females.

Prime Minister Gladstone

In May 1856, when Queen Victoria distributed the first Victoria Crosses at Hyde Park to troops who had distinguished themselves in the Crimean War, she was told of the Sepoy Mutiny in India. The chief cause was that British officers had instructed Hindu and Muslim soldiers ("sepoys"/"sipahis") to tear off the hand grenades laced with beef (objectionable to Hindus) and pork (objectionable to Hindus and to Muslims) fat. Victoria complained of the "cruel suspense" of the probability that much British blood and Indian blood too were going to be shed in India. Victoria was an impatient woman as it was, and the slow transmission of information and details did not help calm her nerves. Victoria kept pushing Prime Minister Lord Palmerston to help secure the "defenseless state" of the United Kingdom in the aftermath of post-Crimea military retrenchments. Suddenly, the tax reduction plan had to be shelved.

More bad news was to come. Word arrived that the commander-in-chief of forces in India, General George Anson, had been murdered by the Indian sepoy rebels; he had in fact died of cholera, though the mutiny was in full force all around the Delhi region in northern India (now known endearingly as the rustic "cow belt"). The Prime Minister quickly sent Sir Colin Campbell to India to fight for Britain. Sir Colin's government would dethrone "the King of Delhi" (a British term of art to undermine the authority of the Mughal Emperor).

Under Victoria's watchful eye, the British Empire would slip from business (the East India Company's merchant control over India) to regency (the British authorities "protecting" the

Mughal Emperor in Delhi) to, ultimately, direct rule over India, the brightest jewel in Victoria's Crown. Victoria had very little idea about how wars are fought and the relevant logistics, and to an extent Albert's naivete could also be blamed for allowing Victoria to state in so blasé a fashion, "Our troops are sure to remain victorious against the Sepoys in the open field, if numbers be not too disproportionate, if they be not badly led, or physically reduced by sickness or fatigue." Restating the obvious, again with naivete, the Queen continued by assuring that the hard part would be for Sir Colin "to try to get a proper 'ensemble' into the military movements, and this will hardly be the case unless an army be formed at Calcutta strong enough to operate from thence with certainty upon the parts of the country in revolt."

Queen Victoria's note of admonition seemed almost like a mother telling the children in the nursery to play nicely and considerately with the neighbourhood children: "Our military reinforcements, [units] dropping in one by one, run the risk of being cut up by being sent on to relieve the different stray columns in distress." These issues were insignificant when considering the Prime Minister's responsibility to the Indian Government. Victoria then argued that Palmerston's unworried approach did not assuage her concern "that the first [reinforcements] which were dispatched [other than soldiers deployed in China] will arrive only in October? The time lost in the arrangements . . . brought their departure to July. There will be, therefore, two whole months . . . when the Indian Government will get no relief whatever, while fighting, marching, &c., lose . . . often as much as 500 men in a day." We should not make the mistake of thinking that this manner of royal intervention in the military was acceptable at the time. It was not. Queen Victoria, because of compliant Prime Ministers or the force of her personality or arguments, or a combination of these factors, just got away with it all.

"[T]he magnitude of the crisis," the Queen argued, was too large for the British Government to suddenly economize. Then she stunned Palmerson by stating that "[f]inancial difficulties don't exist; . . . and this appears hardly the moment to make savings on the Army [budget] estimates." She had got him right where she wanted him, and then she recited the laundry list of indignities and failings of Palmerson's government: "mismanagement, incompetence, penuriousness, confused responsibility, and indifference, already the source of national embarrassment in the Crimea," and now the Indian disaster. The East India Company, since the days of the Tudors in the sixteenth century, was exercising its prerogatives under the royal charter. It was now giving up its authority to the Crown and to the Parliament in Westminster. The Company owned land and collected taxes in India and ran the great show that was the British army in India. The Company was eventually appointed an overseer in London and of course the Governor General who was formally a Company employee was really beholden to the Prime Minister.

There is some doubt as to how much Victoria was being told about the situation in India. She was not a cruel or racist woman — she would indulge in Indian habits and would import Indian man-servants, most notably the servant Abdul, who would install a "Durbar Room" at her Osborne House residence — but her outbursts in favour of crushing the mutiny with a take-no-prisoners approach gives today's readers some pause and perhaps consternation. In December 1857, when the mutiny was decisively crushed, the Queen wrote to Lady Canning, the Governor-

General's wife, "Thank God! Lucknow is saved!"

Was it? Thousands upon thousands of Indians as well as British officers and their families were killed. Villages were ransacked. And in its wake, a post-French Revolution guillotine-type atmosphere, which saw the hanging of everyone from princes to ordinary Indians, was set up. Even the favorite sons of the last Mughal Emperor were killed for treason — a curious charge since "treason" can only be against a legitimate authority and the British had never, out of convenience, previously argued that they were the authorities running India.

Parliamentary legislation to co-opt India through a Viceroy received Victoria's assent on August 2, 1858. The jubilant Queen wrote to Lord Canning, upon whom she conferred an earldom, that this change on behest of "that enormous Empire which is so bright a jewel of her Crown" was indeed "a source of great satisfaction and pride." In 1869, Victoria would authorize the Government to purchase the Suez Canal from the Emir of Cairo, by borrowing from Baron de Rothschild. This subcontinent would endure a messy carve-up in 1947, when the British would leave for good. Communal tension, mainly between Muslims and Hindus, had always been rife and complicated. In 1947, two arms of British India would be cut off and would become Pakistan for the Muslims and a secular India for everyone (including Muslims). In 1971, Pakistan itself would be carved up into the Islamic Republic of Pakistan (to the west) and the Bengali-speaking Bangladesh (to the east). Victorian ambitions directly led to these events, which continue to have geopolitical consequences today. Still, the Queen-Empress would also become mother to her Indian subjects, and the sense of adoration and even vicarious nostalgia remain on the subcontinent for the Victorian era and its queen.

Concerning colonial Africa, the Queen when meeting the deposed Zulu chieftain Cetewayo would impress him greatly by her charm even though she was his captor. In the interesting words of Sir Theophilus Shepstone, the chieftain had to be forced "to submit to the rule of civilisation" after the British and Boer forces had taken over Zulu lands. Victoria told Cetewayo that she "recognised in him a great warrior, who had fought against us, but rejoiced we were now friends." Cetewayo even gave the aging monarch a royal Zulu salute, accepting her suzerainty. Later, to a journalist, the chieftain would say of Queen Victoria, "She is born to rule men. She is like me. We are both rulers. She was very kind to me and I will always think of her."

In the southern part of Africa, the British had been having difficulties with the Boers (Dutch settlers), who wanted African mineral-rich lands and wanted to establish colonies they called the Transvaal Republic and the Orange Free State. Once gold and diamonds were discovered in the Boer Witswatersrand, British landowners fought the Boers for control, and finally Gladstone relented in giving the lands back. In 1895, the Queen would be compelled to ask her Prime Minister to review British legal status in the Transvaal, due to the complications occurring there. It is here in the southern part of Africa that many suspect the seeds of the British Empire's decline first began to take root. It is also here that a young Indian lawyer named Mohandas Karamchand Gandhi would flag the second-class citizenship rights under the apartheid regime of South Africa. Gandhi would take this message to his native India and in 1947 lead India to political autonomy away from Britain.

By the late 19th century, Africa had become the playground for European powers to flaunt their might. However, the gains, which took the form of national pride and access to raw materials, would often be offset by the high costs. A prominent example had been Egypt and the Sudan, where native rebellions threatened to throw out the British, who had themselves ejected the French from the region. In 1884, General Charles Gordon, a legendary hero of the Crimea as well as the Taiping Rebellion in Shanghai, China, went to Africa with the Prime Ministerial and Royal mandate to crush the slave trade in the Upper Nile.

Gordon

Gordon's job was to evacuate every single British resident, down to the last man, woman and child, from Khartoum, where the British were under direct threat by Sudanese mutineers. These rebels were under the leadership of a Muslim mystic known as the Mahdi. Gordon arrived too late and without adequate help, and on January 26, 1885, the Sudanese murdered the British, finally and in a macabre way displaying Gordon's head on a pike. Since Prime Minister Gladstone had failed to send resources on time, the Queen leaked her annoyance to the general public. In 1898, the Mahdist forces would be defeated, decisively, by an army officer named Sir Horatio Kitchener. The great war leader Winston Churchill, then just a youthful imperialist, would be in Kitchener's command. British dominance was never gone for long.

By the 1880s, the length of the Queen's reign began to be celebrated just as much as the substance of it, and 1887 marked the 50th year of her reign. With the elderly Queen's Golden Jubilee coming up, the Palace and its machine were now engaged in an enormous public relations campaign to make the Queen seem like a feminist, something she very clearly had never been. Yet the author Henry Adams' book *Celebrated Women of the Victorian Era* highlighted Victoria's character as one which "which all English girls may well do their best to imitate, and a life which, in their lowlier spheres, they may rightly attempt to follow. Her moral courage, her fortitude, her industry, her elevation of aim, and her tenacity of purpose -- these are qualities which they may successfully cultivate, even if they cannot hope to equal the Queen in perspicuity, in soundness of judgment, in breadth of intellectual sympathy, and in artistic feeling. They may take the woman as exemplar, though they cannot approach the Queen."

The trouble was that this book was devoid of any specific examples, although the Queen undoubtedly was the most prominent woman in public life anywhere in the world. Victoria also enjoying emanating the vibe of being sensible and cool-headed, which was made possible only because her private outbursts were not made public knowledge by her secretary Sir Henry Ponsonby. In *Ethics of the Dust* (1866), an instructive textbook for young girls, John Ruskin highlights "the simplicity and good housewifery of the Queen at Balmoral", when "some time ago, one of the little princesses having in too rough play torn the frock of one of her companions (a private gentleman's daughter), the Queen did not present the young lady with a new frock, but made the princess darn the torn one."

Regardless of any attempted spin, the longevity of Victoria's life and reign were enough reason for the British to celebrate, which they did in style. On 20 June 1887, Victoria began her day in a less than celebratory manner, eating breakfast aside the grave of her beloved Albert, before heading by train to Buckingham for a royal banquet that night. The celebration began in earnest there, as Victoria feasted with 50 foreign kings and princes, along with countless officials from across the empire. Victoria noted in her diary:

"Had a large family dinner. All the Royalties assembled in the Bow Room, and we dined in the Supper-room, which looked splendid with the buffet covered with the gold plate. The table was a large horseshoe one, with many lights on it.

"The King of Denmark took me in, and Willy of Greece sat on my other side. The Princes were all in uniform, and the Princesses were all beautifully dressed. Afterwards we went into the Ballroom, where my band played."

The following day marked the public celebrations of the Golden Jubilee. On 21 June, Victoria began the festivities by traveling in an open landau to Westminster Abbey, with an escort of Indian cavalry. Following the Queen was a seemingly never-ending parade of soldiers who marched past the throngs lined up on the street, many of whom were sitting on benches that had been created just for the celebration. It was said the benches alone stretched nearly 10 miles long. of soldiers in one colour, then another, marched past the spectators, who were accommodated on terraced benches along 10 miles of scaffolding erected for the purpose. Though the procession was a symbol of British magnificence, the queen herself wore a simplistic outfit consisting of a bonnet and a long dress, deciding to eschew a crown.

A depiction of a thanksgiving service on 21 June 1887 in Westminster Abbey celebrating the Golden Jubilee of Queen Victoria, by William Ewart Lockhard

This procession attracted everyone from everyday Britons to colonists and foreign dignitaries. Even curious onlookers attended the procession, including famed American novelist Mark Twain, who wrote that Victoria's procession "stretched to the limit of sight in both directions." Twain also noted the fancy ceremonial attire worn by many of the attendees, clearly not used to such scenes in America.

After she returned to her palace, Victoria made a public appearance on the balcony to huge ovations before retiring to the ballroom, where she handed out Jubilee brooches. Another banquet was held that evening, and this time Victoria was resplendent in a gown embroidered with silver roses, thistles and shamrocks. After being greeted by a countless number of foreign dignitaries, Victoria took in a public fireworks display.

Victoria's Diamond Jubilee Photograph

In 1896, Victoria earned the distinction of becoming the longest reigning monarch in Britain's history, but the 77 year old insisted that public celebrations be held off for that milestone so that everything could culminate with the following year's Diamond Jubilee, which marked her 60th year as queen.

When 20 June 1897 came, Victoria noted in her diary, "How well I remember this day 60 years ago when I was called from my bed by dear Mama to receive the news of my accession." Victoria began the celebration at Windsor Castle before attending a thanksgiving service at St. George's Chapel in Windsor. At the same time, similar services were held across the United

Kingdom, most of which featured a hymn written just for the Jubilee, "O King of Kings" by the Bishop of Wakefield. The following night, another large royal banquet was held by the Queen, and a reception followed in the ballroom. Victoria took note of the decorations for the following day's public festivities in her diary on 21 June, "The streets were beautifully decorated, also the balconies of the houses, with flowers, flags and draperies of every hue."

As with the Golden Jubilee, the public celebrations took place on a day after the actual anniversary, with 22 June (a Tuesday) being officially commemorated as a festival at the behest of Colonial Secretary Joseph Chamberlain. While public parades and receptions were held across the empire in honour of the Jubilee, the Queen's procession included representatives from across the empire. Victoria then held another large procession through London "for the purpose of seeing Her People and of Receiving their Congratulations on having attained the Sixtieth Anniversary of Her Majesty's Reign". As Victoria made her way to St. Paul's Cathedral, she was accompanied by 17 carriages in total, which carried members of her family, royalty from across the world, and numerous envoys, ambassadors and military officers. After a short service, she made her way throughout London, on a route that took her across London Bridge and Westminster Bridge.

That night, Victoria wrote down in her diary, "A never to be forgotten day. No one ever, I believe, has met with such an ovation as was given to me, passing through those 6 miles of streets, including Constitution Hill. The crowds were quite indescribable and their enthusiasm truly marvellous and deeply touching. The cheering was quite deafening and every face seemed to be filled with joy."

Chapter 8: Victoria's Legacy

Incapacitated by a series of small strokes, Queen Victoria died on January 22, 1901, four and a half years after her 1896 Diamond Jubilee. She had ostensibly departed with the Victorian era and its moral code still intact, which would come to take on a life of its own in public memory. Victorian morality has become notorious for its most prude practices, such as the refusal to say "leg" in front of a woman because it was too racy. As a result of the Victorian era's consternation with explicit displays of love in deed or word, the "language of flowers" was used to convey feelings, and even today red roses symbolize love, yellow roses indicate friendship, and pink roses suggest affection.

While there is no doubt that the era was traditionalist and conservative, and its queen strove to be a moral example, the perception of the Victorian era has become a bit extreme. And it's ironic that the woman who has come to symbolize the period was not at all stodgy. While nobody would accuse Victoria of being bawdy, the queen herself drew what would be considered erotic depictions of the male figure and even offered one up to Albert as a present. Victoria continues to be depicted in pop culture as the stately, humorless grandmother, but those who knew her saw her more human side.

Whatever the extent of the Victorian era's moral codes, the fact is that Victoria's simplistic worldview of plain values and rigid loyalties did not endure. Nor did Victoria's sense of buttoned-up morality. The accession of Victoria's son King Edward would see to the end of that by then dated ethos. Victorian morality, and even the era itself, quickly became a relic of the past that came to be viewed with a tinge of nostalgia, but Victoria set forth a standard of royal behavior against which every monarch and member of the Royal Family would be measured. Her beloved Balmoral would become the testing ground of royals, as well as politicians who, as her Prime Minister, Benjamin Disraeli once put it, had to come up "six miles north of civilization." Victoria's beloved grandson George V would revert back to the Victorian ethos, making this the harbinger of the public's rejection of King Edward VIII (George's eldest son and Victoria's great-grandson) and his married American mistress Mrs. Wallis Simpson. Victoria, through her antics and even her erratic behavior, nonetheless formed a closeness and bond with her peoples worldwide that gave her the stature of mother. She remains alive and well in people's memory, having successfully tapped the pulse of her people in a way that few ever have.

Made in the USA
Lexington, KY
15 October 2014